MAKING PAPER
and FABRIC RUBBINGS

MAKING PAPER and FABRIC RUBBINGS

Capturing Designs
from Brasses, Gravestones,
Carved Doors, Coins
and More

Cecily Barth Firestein

Lark Books

DEDICATION

To my husband, who has unfailingly encouraged my artistic efforts.

Editor: Deborah Morgenthal
Art Director and Production: Elaine Thompson
Production Assistant: Hannes Charen
Editorial Assistant: Heather Smith
Photography: Richard Babb
Cover Design: Dana Irwin

Library of Congress Cataloging-in-Publication Data
Firestein, Cecily Barth.
    Making paper and fabric rubbings : capturing designs from brasses,
gravestones, carved doors, coins, and more / by Cecily Barth Firestein.
        p.   cm.
    Includes index.
    ISBN 1-57990-104-2
    1. Rubbing.   2. Paper work.   3. Textile crafts.   I. Title.
TT912.F55   1998
760--dc21   98-37318
                                    CIP

10 9 8 7 6 5 4 3 2 1

First Edition

Published by Lark Books
50 College St.
Asheville, NC 28801, US

©1999, Cecily Barth Firestein

Additional photo credits:
Chinese rubbings, page 12, reprinted, by permission, from *Die Weisheit Der Kunst*,
Gerhard Pommeranz-Liedtke, © Erschienen Im Insel-Verlag, 1963.

Distributed by Random House, Inc., in the United States, Canada,
the United Kingdom, Europe, and Asia

Distributed in Australia by Capricorn Link (Australia) Pty Ltd.,
P.O. Box 6651, Baulkham Hills Business Centre, NSW 2153, Australia

Distributed in New Zealand by Tandem Press Ltd., 2 Rugby Rd.,
Birkenhead, Auckland, New Zealand

Printed in Hong Kong

All rights reserved.

ISBN 1-57990-104-2

Since early childhood I have been painting and "doing art," but for the past 30 years printmaking has been, and still is, my medium of choice. In 1972 I became acquainted with rubbings and incorporated them into my printmaking vocabulary.

Actually my introduction to the realm of rubbings makes an amusing story. An artist friend of mine telephoned to inquire if I'd be interested in teaching a course in rubbings on Saturday mornings, at Fordham University's Lincoln Center campus in New York where I live. She explained that it was to be a special workshop for young people and their parents. I explained that I never heard of rubbings, so how could I possibly teach such a course? She replied, "This is Tuesday. I made you an appointment for an interview on Thursday morning." Then she hung up. Of course, she knew me very well, and knew she had excited my curiosity. I had always enjoyed teaching, and had taught art before, so I wasn't coming from left field completely. As luck would have it, little had been written about rubbings, but by the time I appeared for the interview, I was an expert in the subject. I was accepted as a teacher in the fine art of making rubbings.

Medallion set into the Pilgrim's Pavement in the nave of the Cathedral Church of Saint John the Divine, New York City

The workshop was called the Hopi Workbench, and the brochure stated: "The Hopi Indians, enjoying a strong sense of community, integrated artistic crafts with every phase of village life. This program wishes to celebrate this tradition and restructure the role of the artist in the community. Toward this end, we have gathered together a few of the most creative professional artists in our city to conduct workshops which will add a new dimension to the young person's urban experience."

The class, as it turned out, consisted of small children and their divorced daddies. The dads needed a Saturday morning project and this was an ideal situation for learning and having fun with their children. Because rubbings can be successfully done by anyone with equally good results, it can be a shared, noncompetitive endeavor. We met each Saturday at a preselected site in one of the five boroughs of New York City to "lift rubbings" from architectural details of buildings. The dads and their kids learned about history and architecture and had a good time doing it.

My workshop continued for two years until the Hopi Workbench program ended. At this point

Bronze door at the Bronx County Courthouse, New York

Gate from the old Paramount Building, Collection, Brooklyn Museum

I was really very enthusiastic about the craft of rubbing, and hoped I could find another cultural institution to sponsor similar classes. I approached a staff member at the Museum of the City of New York, thinking that it would be the ideal organization for such a course. The museum official said that if I could fill a class, the museum would support it. I sent flyers advertising the course to all the magazines and, as luck would have it, *New York Magazine* featured it in their "Best Bets." The result was that the course had a three-year waiting list.

The rest, as they say, is history! I've been writing and conducting workshops ever since. I presented many tours for historical and preservation societies which were incredibly well attended. I even conducted a rubbing tour of an old movie theater, The Loew's Paradise, and another at the Wood-lawn Cemetery for the Bronx County Historical Society. It was during this time that I was nick-named "The Pied Piper of Rubbings" and "The Rubber Baroness."

Author "lifting a rubbing" at the Hartsdale Canine Cemetery in New York

WHAT EXACTLY IS A RUBBING?

Before you read further, however, I would like to give you a general explanation of what rubbings are. Lifting a rubbing (the least ambiguous term) is a method of reproducing the surface of a carved or textured design by rubbing or dabbing a piece of

paper or cloth with various media. The process is an extension of what you did as a child when you placed a penny under a sheet of paper and went over the surface with a pencil.

Rubbing allows you to explore the architecture, history, and specific art forms of any city. You can produce an original piece of art from a visit

to an ancient site. Rubbing is also an excellent tool in landmark preservation projects. Since much old stonework is rapidly eroding due to air pollution or is being destroyed by urban redevelopment, lifting a rubbing helps to keep a record of beautiful objects that might otherwise be forgotten.

Old gravestone, Trinity Churchyard, New York City

On all these tours, working with novices in the art of lifting rubbings, everyone went home with a prize—a beautiful rubbing suitable for framing. I emphasize here that anyone, of almost any age, can complete a handsome rubbing; the process requires no artistic ability, doesn't take much time, and is easy and inexpensive to do. When a rubbing has been completed and you step back a few paces to admire it, the pleasure is similar to what the artist must have felt when he produced the original object years before.

This enthusiasm for the craft of rubbing, along with the favorable response to my first book *Rubbing Craft*, has led me to write this new book, which expands upon the subject. In this book, I emphasize the enhanced pleasure of travel when you bring along your rubbing supplies, and how much fun and educational joy children experience by participating in this art form.

Art Deco door panel from the Dollar Savings Bank, Bronx, New York

Decorative as well as functional objects can be rubbed. Art Deco forms cover many urban build-ings and make lovely rubbings. You can find many periods of art and architecture in large cities that

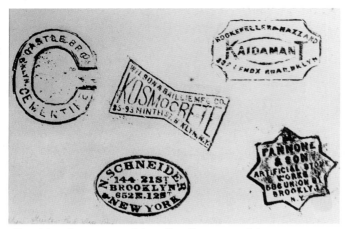

Advertising plaques cemented into sidewalks, at turn of the century, in Park Slope section of Brooklyn.

explore rubbing on fabric. Potentially, all objects up to about a half inch in depth can be transferred to paper or fabric through rubbing. Different techniques facilitate the process. You can lift a rubbing from the side of a building or from the surface of an interesting button, coin, or beautiful leaf. This book will tell you everything you ever wanted to know about the lifting of rubbings, as well as offer you dozens of projects that make use of the finished rubbing or the design itself. So grab some paper, a few crayons, and your imagination, and I'll meet you out on the streets!

can provide you with a wealth of subjects from which to lift rubbings. Look down at the dated, turn-of-the-century sewer covers in the streets or at the historical plaques in the sidewalk. Look up at the wrought-iron window guards or the numerals over a doorway. Don't miss the elegant raised surfaces of some church doors. If you keep your eyes open, it's easy to find unlimited subject matter for this wide-ranging craft.

Generally, rubbings are done with paper and colored crayons, inks, or graphite paste. In this book, I also

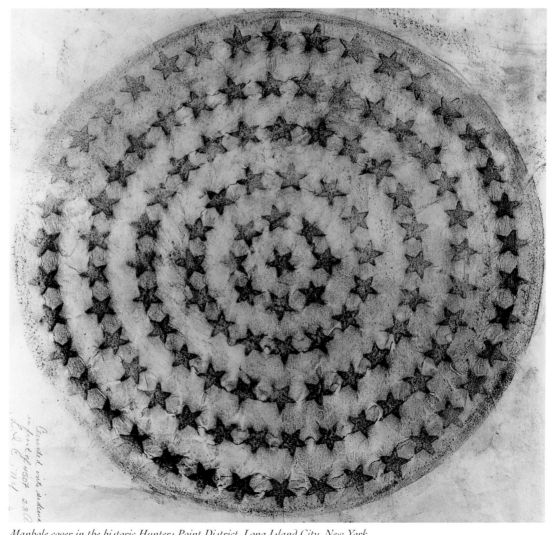

Manhole cover in the historic Hunters Point District, Long Island City, New York

The term *rubbing* is technically used to describe the ancient Chinese technique known as *T'a-pen* or *ink squeeze*. Basically, a piece of paper (generally rice paper) is placed over the surface to be reproduced. The paper is then rubbed with crayon, graphite, or ink to produce a negative image. The resulting print is called a rubbing.

CHINESE ORIGINS

Although the oldest known stone rubbing in existence dates from the seventh century A.D., it is believed that rubbings or "stone prints" were employed in China as early as 300 B.C. Used by the ancients as a kind of reporting or journalistic technique before the invention of the printing press, calligraphic messages were carved upon stones and placed in central areas. Travelers passing through could make rubbings of the news and then return to their communities to post the news there. During the Ch'in dynasty (221 to 206 B.C.) the Chinese incised inscriptions directly onto rocks as well as onto stone stele or slabs. These carvings commemorated various undertakings, such as travels, military exploits, and biographies of important persons. In A.D. 175, Ling Ti, the emperor of the Eastern Han Dynasty, ordered seven stone slabs to be erected in front of the imperial academy. He ordered carvers to inscribe them with the Seven Confucian Classics, and then he had a scholar, Ts'ai Yung, copy these inscriptions by hand. This was the first attempt to disseminate a message to

Chinese rubbing of Buddha

a mass audience. Paper had already been invented in China at this time, and the traditional method of reproducing inscriptions was to hand-copy the text onto bamboo strips that were strung together with cord. With the emergence of the "stone classics," it became feasible to spread messages by means of rubbing. This approach was much faster then the hand-copying method.

Pictorial stone carvings were also made in ancient China for the sole purpose of being reproduced by rubbing. During the Ming period, books were published from rubbings. Because it was sometimes

Above and right: Chinese rubbings

difficult for Asians to visit graves, those living closer to these sites made rubbings of the grave-stones to present to relatives. According to Thomas Carter, in his book, *The Invention of Printing in China and Its Spread Westwards*, classics of the T'ang dynasty were cut in stone, and people were appointed to make rubbings from them. The Chinese method of lifting rubbings was to place moistened paper on the inscription, and then to force the paper into the incised lines with a stiff brush. When the paper dried, a tamper of silk was touched to Sumi ink and then dabbed evenly over the surface of the paper. The paper was then removed, producing a white-on-black-background replica of the inscription. The Chinese still assign people to lift rubbings from classical slabs and carvings. These rubbings can be purchased extensively and inexpensively at souvenir shops throughout China.

GYOTAKU

In the mid-17th century, rubbings spread to Japan, where they were executed primarily in the form of *gyotaku*. This is a wet technique used to make impressions of fish. The Chinese calligraphic character for gyotaku is fish; the phonetic sound "gyo" is pronounced with a hard "G," as in the German name Goethe. I mention this because if the word gyotaku is mispronounced, using a "G" as in "George," the word has a completely different connotation and may prove embarrassing. It is still a rubbing but specifies the anatomy of a woman. (I learned this the hard way after two Japanese ladies in a class I was teaching laughed so hard there were tears in their eyes; they came up to me after class to explain.) The other Chinese character means "stone monument rubbing," and that is pronounced "taku."

Gyotaku is also appropriate for recording other natural forms such as leaves, flowers, seaweed, star fish, shell fish, shrimp, seashells, butterflies, crabs, and tree bark. The technique requires painting the object itself and then pressing and molding rice paper to that form with pressure from your fingers. Painting the object itself is both a defacing and destructive method when dealing with the built environment, but is certainly suitable when dealing with inanimate forms in nature.

Japanese rubbing

13

MONUMENTAL BRASSES AND BRASS RUBBINGS

A many of our bodies shall no doubt
Find native graves; upon the which I trust
Shall witness lives in brass of this day's work:
And those that leave their valiant bones in France,
Dying like men, though buried in your dunghills,
They shall be fam'd. . . .
       Henry V, Act IV, Scene 3 by William Shakespeare

In the West, lifting rubbings is a relatively recent tradition. It was, and still is, actively pursued in England, where residents and visitors have long enjoyed lifting rubbings from monumental brasses, which first appeared in England during the late 13th century. These brass plaques, engraved with figures, inscriptions, and decorations, commemorate the deceased, and were laid down in great numbers in English churches. Traditional brass rubbings were done using black wax on white paper. More recently, gold wax on black paper has become popular.

English brass monuments differed from those produced on the Continent, being less ornate, with concentration on the human figure. The figure's costume was generally consistent with the period, although faces did not necessarily depict the person commemorated. It was not until the Elizabethan period that portraiture became significant.

Cast brass sheets were popular in western Europe beginning in the 12th century. The earliest known brass memorial plaque is in Verden, Germany, and commemorates Bishop Yso Wilpe, who died in 1231. Brasses were also produced in France, Belgium, Flanders, Italy,

Switzerland, Poland, and the Scandinavian countries. Lists of the locations of these brasses are available in the definitive book on the subject by Henry Trivick, entitled *The Craft and Design of Monumental Brasses* (John Baker, 1969).

Facsimile Brasses

The incentive for producing facsimiles of the monumental brasses developed from the concern of the clergy that too many enthusiastic people were lifting rubbings of the brasses in their churches. They feared damage to both the brasses and the stones into which they were set. It is now almost impossible to get permission to rub the originals, and this has led to the practice of providing the churches with replicas of their brasses so that visitors can lift rubbings. A mail-order rubbing supply company, Whitewinds, located in England, simulates the original brasses by using powdered brass and granite chippings to produce their molds. When a rubbing is made using one of these facsimiles it is almost impossible to distinguish it from a rubbing lifted from the original brass.

Brass facsimile rubbing from the Brass Rubbing Centre, London

Left: Brass facsimile rubbing from the Brass Rubbing Centre,, London

Above: Sir John de Creke and his wife Alyne, Westley Waterless, Cambridgeshire, 1325

Above right: Brass facsimile of Sir William de Setvans, Chartham, Kent, 1322

Another development arising from the accessibility of these reproductions has been the opening of brass rubbing centers. These are extremely popular throughout England, and are replete with all required supplies, and even assistance (for a fee). They tend to be located in the basements of churches. The London Brass Rubbing Centre, for example, is located in the crypt of the Church of Saint Martin-in-the-Field at Trafalgar Square. You may also purchase completed rubbings and all variety of souvenirs with rubbings imprinted on them. Both centers are listed in the source list on page 106.

GRAVESTONE RUBBINGS

In America, the most popular places for lifting rubbings are cemeteries, particularly very old ones in New England. Early Puritan burying grounds, with their stone slabs and well-known designs, are reflections of the religious beliefs of the time. The earliest grave markers were simply field stones with the deceased's initials carved on them. By the middle of the 1600s, stone cutters were using stones smoothed on one side to facilitate carving. The predominant motifs on the stones are death heads, urns and willows, and the soul effigy. By the 18th century, these tombstones were embellished with

A HISTORY LESSON: WALTER JUDAH'S GRAVESTONE

In 1974, I received a grant from the New York State Preservation League to form a tangible record, through rubbings, of all the ancient gravestones in the three Jewish cemeteries belonging to the Spanish-Portuguese Congregation (Shearith Israel). Pollution was producing deterioration of the stones, and their legends were becoming increasingly illegible.

In the Chatham Square Cemetery, the oldest Jewish cemetery in the United States, in use from 1682 to 1831, I came across the tombstone of a certain Walter Judah. It was both the unusual carved composition on the stone and the legibility of the epitaph which aroused my curiosity concerning the man buried beneath. The scene on the upper portion of the stone depicts the New York City skyline as viewed from the East River. An angel's arm is cutting down a young tree while an angel of destruction holds a sword over Manhattan.

From family records, it is substantiated that Walter Jonas Judah was a medical student who died aiding people during the Yellow Fever Epidemic in New York City in 1798. Yellow Fever was, at that time, thought to be a contagious disease. Doctors attending patients were

considered courageous and heroic. Sixteen physicians died during that one epidemic in New York City, a number which translates to approximately 40 percent of the practicing physicians in Manhattan. It was not until 1901 that scientists confirmed that Yellow Fever is transmitted by mosquitoes. In 1939, Max Theiler, a South African physician, developed the vaccine which gave immunity to those exposed to the disease.

The gravestone reads:

In Memory of

Walter J. Judah

Student of Physic, who worn down by his Exertions to

Alleviate the

Sufferings of his Fellow Citizens

In that Dreadful Contagion

That visited the City of New York

In 1798 Fell a Victim in the Cause

Of Humanity the 5th of Tishri

A.M. 5559 Corresponding

with the 15th of September 1798

AET 20 Years 5 Months

and 11 Days

Here lies buried / The unmarried man - - - - / Old in wisdom, tender in years / Skilled he was in his labor, the labor of healing / Strengthening himself as a lion and running swiftly as a hart to bring healing / To the inhabitants of this city treating them with loving kindness / When they were visited with the yellow-fever / He gave money from his own purse to buy for them beneficent medicines / But the good that he did was the cause of his death / For the fever visited him while yet a youth in his twenty-first year / Declare him and his soul happy / May they prepare for him his canopy in Paradise / And there may he have refreshment of soul until the dead live again and the spirit reenter into them / Joshua the son of Samuel / departed hence / on the holy Sabbath day the 5 of Tishri / In the year 5559 / And thou shalt rest and stand in they lot at the end of the days [Daniel XII, 13]

May his soul be bound up in the bond of life.

more decorative designs, including winged cherubs, hearts, birds, and vines. In and around Massachusetts, facial portraits of the deceased gained popularity. For those interested in the symbolism and craftsmanship of these early markers, *Gravestones of Early New England and the Men Who Made Them* (1853–1800), written by Harriette Merrifield Forbes, sheds a great deal of light on the subject through photographs and scholarly research. Cemeteries the world over are interesting sites from which to lift rubbings, while simultaneously learning a little local history.

Above: Gravestone rubbing, Westminster, Vermont
Below: Detail of old gravestone rubbing, Westminster, Vermont

Other Important Uses for Rubbings

Rubbings are employed in many professions. Archaeologists find rubbings a valuable aid in the reproduction of carved interiors of ancient vessels. Rubbings are made to capture the stories told by symbols used in petroglyphs. Museums sometimes use rubbing techniques when photography is not feasible, as it is sometimes possible to reproduce details by rubbing that are not clear or visible to the eye. Museums use rubbings for displaying delicate collections in an interesting and attractive manner. Fossil rubbings may be done from the original fossil or from casts. Costume designers who are interested in medieval costumery often use brass rubbings for reference. When describing clothing of

this period, costume books use rubbings as illustrations. The Victoria and Albert Museum also offers its *Catalogue of Rubbings of Brasses and Incised Slabs*, which categorizes the brasses into costume types (legal, military, royal, etc.).

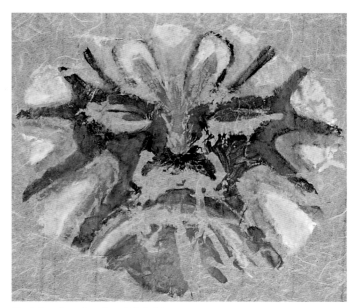

Facial makeup imprint of Kabuki actor

Rubbings from exterior wall at the American Museum of Natural History, New York City

In Japan, Kabuki actors are viewed as rock stars, and have throngs of admiring fans who want personal souvenirs from them. Often an actor will press tissue-thin rice paper to his face to create an imprint of the Kabuki makeup. This image (rubbing) is then presented to his admirer.

However, you don't need to travel far to make a visually, and, perhaps historically interesting, rubbing. Just visit the cemetery of a local church; if the churchyard is an old one, you'll be likely to find handsome gravestones to rub, replete with cryptograms, skull and crossbones, hearts and cherubs. Or walk around your own town with an observant gaze: you may be surprised at how many carved designs on buildings or doors you suddenly see that would make terrific rubbings.

TEACHING HISTORY THROUGH RUBBING

The built environment presents a fascinating array of details that most people ignore as they pass. The

lifting of rubbings draws this world into sharper focus, stimulates active observation of the environment, encourages direct experience with forms and textures, and makes history a part of today's life.

I recently saw a "do and learn" project at El Museo del Barrio in East Harlem, New York, that I thought was particularly innovative. A small room was set aside for an exhibition of petroglyphs from the Caribbean. In the center of the room was a platform with a large map on it, with markers pointing to where each petroglyph was located. A string was attached from each marker to a replica of a petroglyph. Paper and pencils were supplied and the children happily made rubbings of the petroglyphs while learning about the region and its history. Personal, fun, and inter-active experiences with history can encourage children to learn about the past.

Children, even very young ones, can produce satisfactory rubbings as easily as adults. Making rubbings of sites with historical importance is a pleasant and productive way for adults and children to spend time together. Before embarking on any endeavor of this sort, be sure to obtain permission from the relevant authority in charge.

EXPLORING ART FORMS

Lifting rubbings also offers the opportunity for you to explore art forms, as well as the architectural and decorative history of a city, or even of a particular building. For example, in New York City's Central Synagogue (1872), with its Moorish Revival interior, the entire vestibule was embellished with embossed wallpaper. As I lifted rubbings of that paper several years ago, little did I suspect that these rubbings would be the sole record of the original decorative covering; it has since been covered over with a plastic foam finish. Because of periodic repairs through the years, the surface was made up of four different patterns, seemingly similar, and all painted over with the same uniform beige. Each generation of congregants repaired the wall covering with what they thought to be a similar pattern. Rubbing brought all these patterns to light. The earliest was a simple floral spray, followed by an art nouveau floral, and then two later papers with simpler versions of the floral motif.

Rubbing excursions are an exciting way to reinforce a lesson learned in a history textbook.

A rubbing of the gravestone of Peter Stuyvesant, for example, in the churchyard of St. Mark's, in the Bowery district of

New York City, makes history more believable to children, and provides tangible evidence that the first director general of New York (New Netherlands) actually existed!

Today, England still ranks highest in popularity as a place to lift rubbings, primarily because of the monumental brasses. These brasses provide an excellent overview of English costume, heraldry, armor, and women's fashions. They also provide a look at the development of the English language from the 14th century onwards. But the rubbing you make today in your own city or town may also have the potential to bring history to life.

Embossed wallpaper rubbing from Central Synagogue, New York City

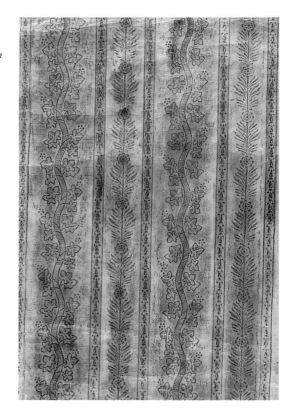

Sir Edward and Lady Cerne, Draycot Cerne, Wilts, 1393

MORE ABOUT MONUMENTAL BRASSES

UNTIL THE 13TH CENTURY, STONE AND MARBLE WERE THE USUAL MATERIALS FOR MONUMENTS, WHICH WERE PLACED WITHIN CHURCHES. ASIDE FROM TAKING UP A GREAT DEAL OF SPACE, THESE CARVED MARKERS WERE WEARING BADLY. WITH THE AVAILABILITY OF BRASS ("LATTEN" OR "LATEN," IT WAS CALLED), MEMORIALS OF THIS MATERIAL BECAME POPULAR. THE ENGRAVING ON THESE PLATES WAS MORE DURABLE, AND SINCE THEY WERE MOUNTED FLAT, EITHER ON WALLS OR FLOORS, THEY TOOK UP LESS SPACE IN CHURCHES. THESE BRASSES WERE NO MORE EXPENSIVE TO PRODUCE THAN STONE OR MARBLE MONUMENTS, AND COULD EVEN BE WALKED UPON WITHOUT APPARENT DAMAGE.

ENGLISH BRASSES EVOLVED FROM INCISED SLAB DESIGNS THAT MADE USE OF BRASS IMPORTED FROM THE CONTINENT. BRASS, A COPPER-ZINC ALLOY, CAN BE FORGED, CAST, OR ROLLED; FOR MEMORIAL BRASSES, CAST SHEETS WERE ORIGINALLY USED. BRASS WAS IMPORTED TO ENGLAND FROM EUROPE UNTIL ELIZABETHAN TIMES, BUT BY THE END OF THE 16TH CENTURY, BRASS WAS BEING PRODUCED BY THE BRITISH. THIS LATTER ALLOY WAS SOMEWHAT DIFFERENT FROM THAT ON THE CONTINENT, AND THE PLATES WERE ROLLED INSTEAD OF CAST. THEY WERE ALSO OF A THINNER BRASS, WHICH AFFECTED THE STYLES.

BY THE END OF THE 14TH CENTURY THERE WERE SCHOOLS OF ENGRAVERS IN ENGLAND. ARTISTS TRANSFERRED DESIGNS TO BRASS PLATES WITH BLACK PAINT OR CHALK. ENGRAVERS THEN EMPLOYED BURINS AND HAMMERS TO CUT AWAY THE SURFACE, LEAVING THE CARVING IN RELIEF. THE LATER, THINNER BRASSES WERE SOMETIMES ETCHED WITH ACID AFTER BEING LIGHTLY INCISED. SMALL RECTANGULAR PLATES BECAME POPULAR, AND WITH ECONOMIC DEPRESSION, PEOPLE CHOSE CHEAPER MATERIALS. THE BRASSES COULD BE MOUNTED WITHOUT STONE CASE-

MENTS, FURTHER REDUCING COSTS. WITH THE REFORMATION, HENRY VIII (1491–1547) BEGAN DESTROYING THE ABBEYS, AND PLUNDERED EVERYTHING OF WORTH, INCLUDING THE BRASSES, WHICH WERE USED FOR OTHER PURPOSES. DURING THE REIGN OF MARY STUART, A CATHOLIC (1516–1558), A RESPITE FROM THIS DESTRUCTION TOOK PLACE. QUEEN ELIZABETH I (1533–1603) ISSUED EDICTS FORBIDDING DAMAGE TO MONUMENTS FOR THE DEAD, AND THIS DID HALT THE LARGE-SCALE DESTRUCTION. BY THE END OF THE 17TH CENTURY COMPARATIVELY FEW MONUMENTAL BRASSES WERE BEING PRODUCED, ALTHOUGH SOME DIMINISHED PRODUCTION DID CONTINUE THROUGH THE 18TH AND EVEN 19TH CENTURIES.

Rubbing of Queen Elizabeth I, London

In addition to learning history from rubbings, children's aesthetics can also develop from this simple activity. A unique method for encouraging this development in young children is simply to have them rub contrasting textural surfaces in their environment. For example, a child can lift a

rubbing from a smooth leaf with prominent veins and then rub some rough gravel in a paved sidewalk. Once children appreciate the basic idea that a rubbing is a pictorial impression of a particular surface, they will become very aware of how many different surfaces are available for rubbing.

Children find textured objects in the most unusual places. They like to rub items from nature, including leaves, bark, flowers, and seashells. Around the house they can lift a rubbing from string, coins, buttons, and food graters. A walk down the street will yield other objects to rub, such as

car license plates, sewer and manhole covers, or numerals of the address on a front door. The list goes on and on!

NECESSARY MATERIALS

The materials that young children need to make these first rubbings are minimal: primary crayons, a large roll of inexpensive paper, such as shelf-lining paper, scissors, and a roll of masking tape. The child simply covers the entire surface of the object to be rubbed with paper, cuts off any excess paper, tapes it down, and rubs the paper with a crayon. Don't worry about how neat the result looks. The idea is to encourage the child to explore textures and have fun doing it.

These first textural rubbings can form the basis of an ongoing collection; they could be mounted in a scrapbook or cut up and organized into a collage. Conversely, a collage can be created from small textured papers, pasted onto a piece of cardboard, and a rubbing made from that creation.

SUBJECTS FOR RUBBING

Leaves and coins can be rubbed onto attractive paper to create a repeat pattern; then the paper can be used as gift-wrapping paper, as was done for the project on page 87. Small rubbings that feature a single item, rubbed with different colored crayons, can be made into attractive greeting cards or bookmarks. Any of these rubbings can be placed on a copy machine and reproduced. Several of the greeting cards with matching envelopes can be tied with a ribbon and given as distinctive gifts.

Another approach is for the child to use white glue to attach yarn, string, and twine onto cardboard. Then she can lift a rubbing using white, gold, or silver crayons on black paper.

Shells and coral are popular subjects for children to rub. The nautilus shell shown here was rubbed  directly from the shell with China marking pencils, Prismacolors, and a watercolor wash on architectural detail paper. For the coral and sand dollar, I used ordinary crayons.

Once children have mastered lifting the most elementary rubbings, they can easily proceed to the various techniques described in this book. I would not attempt the Sumi ink method, however, as this can be frustrating, even for adults. Always keep in mind that you or the child needs to obtain permission if you will be lifting rubbings on property other than your own. Be sure to clean up any mess left behind from this activity. To clean yourself up, always bring along some type of disposable wipes.

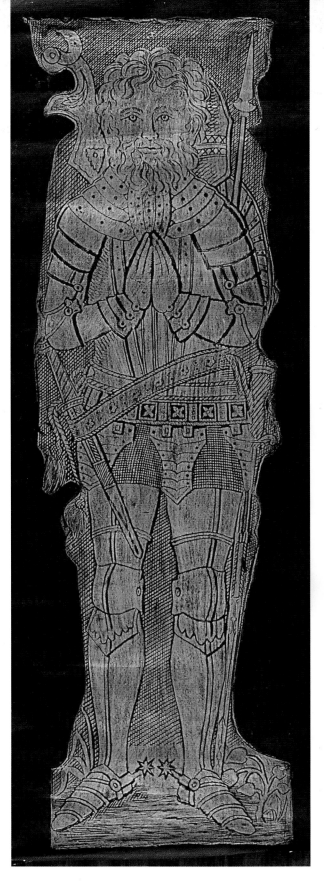

Rubbing from
The Brass Rubbing
Centre, London, England

Frequently I bring home the most remarkable travel souvenirs from places that I visit. They are free, require little effort to obtain, and are lusted after by most people who see them. They are the rubbings that I have lifted from architectural details at locations around the world. Rubbings take only slightly longer to create than photographs and they look more like drawings. Generally it is instant gratification. Once

Author lifting a rubbing in Prambanan, Indonesia

framed, these rubbings may form the basis for an inexpensive as well as unique art collection. Travel rubbings make wonderful gifts to give to friends or to onlookers, who are usually amazed that you have found beauty in objects they pass without special notice in the course of their daily routine.

When I travel, I carry my rubbing supplies in a plastic shopping bag, my belt looped through the handles. One tends to resemble a "bag person," but it is convenient to have your hands free and your materials close by.

THE CHINESE CONNECTION

Lifting rubbings can also spark positive interactions that otherwise may not have taken place. For instance, when I was in China making rubbings, I drew crowds of interested and helpful Chinese spectators who nodded approvingly while I worked. In each city in China that I visited, I made an effort to do rubbings. At the Great Wall, near Beijing, I was amazed to discover the Wall covered with graffiti carved into the stone in Chinese characters. This made for a unique rubbing. I tried my hand at some bas-reliefs at the Ming Tombs and on carvings from the wooden doors of the Summer Palace.

At the Hot Springs in Xian I drew an interested and approving group of onlookers. At this same location I made a small rubbing which I gave to a young boy, delighting both him and me. He was thrilled with the small gift, and I was pleased with his amusement and satisfaction.

The Hua Ting Sheraton Hotel in Shanghai where I stayed, is a monument to modern European architecture in its own right. In front of the hotel I made a rubbing of a manhole cover, collecting quite a crowd, as well as several assistants and supervisors. Many of my observers spoke to me in English, eager to practice what they had learned from their English lessons on television. They posed numerous questions about life in the United States, especially in New York City, and

Above: The author lifting a rubbing of a decorative frieze at the Ming Tombs near Beijing, China

Below: The author rubbing the decorative doors at the Summer Palace near Beijing, China

The author lifts a rubbing of a manhole cover outside a hotel in Shanghai, China

about the rubbing I was lifting of the manhole cover. Some inquired if they could try the technique with my supplies. I agreed, and soon I was surrounded by a group of instant experts.

Even on a tightly organized tour of China I was able to return home with a sizeable collection of rubbings. What a unique gift to bring to the folks back home…a piece of the Great Wall of China in their own back yard…or more literally, a rubbing from the Great Wall that they can display in their own home.

Rubbing in Israel was fascinating, too, especially in the Arab cemetery in Safed, Israel; while rubbing a plaque commemorating a soldier killed in the Six Day War, a woman introduced herself who owned a copy of my previous book!

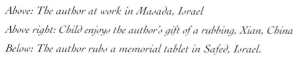

Above: The author at work in Masada, Israel
Above right: Child enjoys the author's gift of a rubbing, Xian, China
Below: The author rubs a memorial tablet in Safed, Israel.
Below right: The finished rubbing

When Things Go Wrong...

On Java Island, where I could not wait to rub the fantastic carvings at Borobodur, the experience was a basic disaster, although a definite learning experience. It is important, psychologically, to be prepared for this type of experience. Sometimes, as in this instance, the qualities of the stone are antithetical to what makes for a good rubbing. The stone at Borobudar was grainy and weathered, and the bas-reliefs were too prominent. It was impossible to get a satisfactory rubbing, no matter what technique I used. I tried the graphite methods, as well as dampened paper with ink and dabbers—all to no avail. I visited Bali on this same trip, and the only clear rubbings I returned home with were of the hand-carved furniture in my hotel room! At least I did find something characteristic of the area.

So be forewarned, bas-reliefs can only be ½ to ¾ inches (1 to 2 cm) deep, and the smoother the surface of the subject, the less problems you will encounter.

The author attempts to make a rubbing of the impressive stone wall at Borobodur, Java Island, Indonesia.

27

Panel from the Great Bronze Doors of the Cathedral Church of Saint John the Divine, New York City

In Memory of William French,
Son to Mr Nathaniel French, Who
Was Shot at Westminster March y^{e} 13th
1775, by the hands of Cruel Ministereal tools
of Georg y^{e} 3^{d} in the Corthouse at a 11 a Clock
at Night in the 22^{d} year of his Age.

Here William French his Body lies.
For Murder his Blood for Vengance cries.
King Georg the third his Tory crew.
tha with a bawl his head Shot threw.
For Liberty and his Countrys Good.
he Lost his Life his Dearest blood.

Left: Tombstone rubbing, Wilmington, Vermont
Above: Tombstone rubbing, Westminster, Vermont

Right: Portrait gravestone rubbing, Marblehead, Massachusetts

Below left: Rubbing from Le Mans Cup Trophy headstone in the Hartsdale Canine Cemetery, New York

Below right: Gravestone rubbing, Vermont

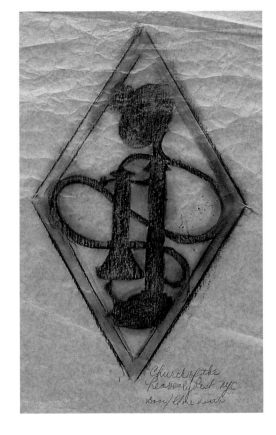

Above: Siamese temple rubbing

Right: Interior Door, phone booth, The Church of the Heavenly Rest, New York City

Below: Brass trim on skyscraper, Chicago

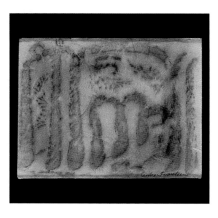

Above: Mamilla Cemetery, Jerusalem

Right: Gravestone rubbing, Woodstock, Vermont

In Memory of
Capt. Israel Richardson
Who died May
7th 1799 Æ 63 y

Left: Detail of old gravestone

Below: Siamese Temple rubbing

Below right: The Alhambra, Grenada, Spain

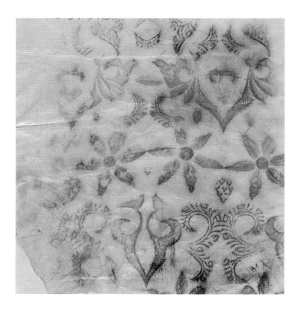

Exterior door/strap hinges from the Church of Heavenly Rest, depicting events in New York City history, New York City

Early wallpaper, Central Synagogue, New York City

Left: Elevator door in the Waldorf Astoria Hotel, New York City

Above: Siamese temple rubbing

Right: Elevator door in the Bronx Country Courthouse, New York

Above: Sewer cover, Central Park, New York City
Far right: Manhole cover, Arab Quarter, Old Jerusalem

41

Right: Old gravestone, Woodlawn Cemetery, Bronx, New York

Below: Detail of wooden grave marker, Quebec, Canada

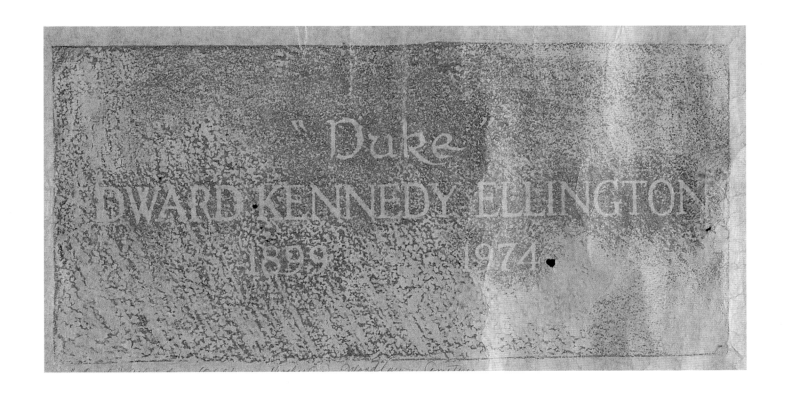

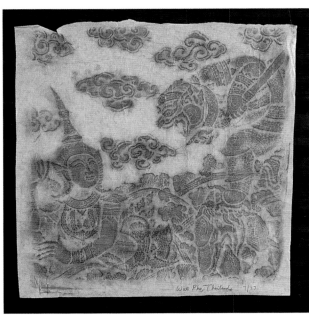

Top: *Duke Ellington's headstone, Woodlawn Cemetery, Bronx, New York*

Above right: *Thai rubbing*

Above left: *Detail of old gravestone*

Linden Hill Cemetery, Central Synagogue, New York

44

Left: Greek Chapel, Church of the Holy Sepulchre, Old Jerusalem

Above: Symbol of St. Mark from the Great Bronze Doors, Cathedral Chrurch of Saint John the Divine, New York City

Rubbing materials include (approximately in rows starting upper left) decorative paper, rubbing paper, silk, Sumi ink (liquid), suzuri (stone plate), beeswax candle, Sumi ink (dry), rubbing waxes, Sumi ink (dry), dauber, lumber crayon, pastel dye sticks, rubbing waxes, graphite powder, brushes, scissors, rubbing waxes, paintbrush, chamois cloth, crayons, rubbing waxes, linen napkin

PAPERS

It is a good idea to experiment with different papers so that you will know firsthand the results they deliver under different situations. There are a great many choices, especially when you are involved with the dry rubbing techniques. If the cost of the paper is a concern, try inexpensive papers, such as brown wrapping paper. If you are a beginner, you can even use paper towels or shelf-lining paper. These cheap papers are also practical to use with small children.

There are problems, however, with these particular papers; they tend to tear while you are rubbing, and some of them are too thick for tracing a somewhat worn or lightly incised surface. Other problems are archival ones; inexpensive papers become brittle and/or turn yellow with time. This could be a problem if you are trying to construct a collection of rubbings over a period of years. It is also upsetting to find that a rubbing you spent a great deal of time on has disintegrated.

An example of an unfortunate choice of paper is pictured below. Many years ago a gentleman

from England sent me this "certified rubbing" from the grave of William Shakespeare. It was

effected in 1944. During the intervening years, I discovered that the paper had yellowed, crumpled, creased, and that a section of the lettering was missing. If a better, more appropriate paper had been employed, the rubbing would still be in excellent condition.

I would like to emphasize that these less durable papers are for practice sessions or for emergencies when no quality paper is available. As you gain confidence, I feel sure you will want to graduate to finer, though more expensive, papers.

Art and Japanese Papers

For the dry, wax crayon technique, many fine art papers are manufactured that are appropriate and aesthetically enhance the rubbing by adding an interesting background or attractive color. Many of these papers, such as a Japanese paper called Moriki (also called Yomato and Yatsuo), comes in white and 25 different colors. This paper is handmade from kozo and sulphite pulp. Kozo is a plant in the mulberry family. Its fibers are comparatively long, which produces a tough paper that neither shrinks or expands. Most Japanese papers are made from mulberry plant fibers, selected because of their strength. Moriki has a strong, soft, laid surface. It is pH neutral and is supplied in sheets approximately 25 x 37 inches (63 x 93 cm). The paper picks up the details of the undersurface when rubbed with wax crayons or heel ball.

Other oriental specialty papers that are appropriate are the lightweight Kozo 436 (100 percent kozo fiber) and Kozo 547. The slightly heavier Mulberry, derived from kozo and sulphite, has an unsized fuzzy surface. Okawara, beige (machine made), comes in large sheets 36 x 72 inches (90 x 180 cm). Okawara student grade, a lighter weight paper, comes in small sheets that measure 13 x 19 inches (33 x 48 cm), perfect to use for a practice sheet.

As an aside, I would like to impart some additional information about kozo papers. Variations in the climate affect the characteristics in the kozo, which in turn changes the personality of the resulting sheets. Kozo papers are often known by the name of the area in Japan from which the fibers originate, as well as by the reputation of the individual paper maker. Certain paper (such as Mino Gami) has been admired since A.D. 702, and is now designated in Japan as an "Important Intangible Cultural Property." Some of the paper makers from this province have been declared "National Living Treasures of Japan" for the exceptional quality of their papers.

Other High-Quality Papers

In general, when minute details are paramount in the finished rubbing, I prefer to use a harder,

Assorted oriental specialty papers: Mulberry, Manilla-shi Olive, Grain, Sujikawashi Buff, Unryu White, and Okawara Student Grade

smoother paper surface. In America, bond paper is excellent for this purpose; Aquabee is a good brand. These papers do not, however, compare to the English papers.

English papers are simply the best for making wax rubbings. Called Brass Rubbing Paper, they come in black and white. They have a high rag content with long strands, and are available primarily in England (refer to the mail-order list on page 106).

Another paper I have found success with is a mold-made, cold-press paper from Germany called Zerkall Book. This white vellum, which measures 24 x 34 inches (60 x 85 cm) is smooth, and contains 25 percent cotton. Another Zerkall book stock

made of high alpha cellulose and cotton is also good and measures 20¾ x 30 inches (54 x 75 cm).

My favorite all-around paper is Aqaba. It performs extremely well in all rubbing techniques, whether you are using wet or dry methods. Aqaba is machine-made in the United States from 100 percent hemp. It is produced for the food industry as a filter paper, and therefore has great wet strength, permitting water to pass through it freely. A variety of this filter paper is used to hold tea, and is made into bags for that purpose. Aqaba paper is available in sheets measuring 24 x 36 inches (60 x 90 cm) and in rolls measuring 60 inches (150 cm) wide and 10 yards (9.15 m) long. For those monumental rubbings you may be planning, this paper is also available in 100-yard (91.5 m) rolls, and comes in white and black. The black paper looks dramatic when used in conjunction with silver, gold, or white rubbing waxes. If Aqaba is not available, try asking for it under the name Royal Rubbing Paper or Tableau. Unfortunately, Aqaba is not an archival paper, but I have not had problems with it standing up well for many years. This is a terrific paper for beginners.

Decorative Papers

It is possible to enrich a rubbing through the use of decorative papers. It is a good idea to experiment with different papers to discover which ones work best when you are lifting a rubbing.

In putting this book together, I tried making rubbings using a variety of decorative papers, and some of the papers definitely were not a good match for rubbings. For instance, Japanese leather flecked tissue paper, machine-made from synthetic fibers, sulphite pulp, and colored leather shavings, was much too fragile and tore easily. Philippine Salago (heavy weight), made from 100 percent palm fiber, was much too thick and did not reveal a clear image. On the other hand, Philippine Salago (lightweight), a textured palm fiber paper, worked well. I liked the unique results of a rubbing I made with wood grain kozo, hand printed from the actual grain of a block of wood. Thai newspaper, machine-made of kozo, with small pieces of Bangkok newspaper embedded in the paper, added an interesting background. Thai kozo and chiri, with its large swirls of long silky fibers and mulberry bark, picked up the rubbed image very well and is decorative in itself. Japanese shadow print paper, with a 100 percent watermarked striped design, also added a distinctive touch to the rubbing, and the image was clear.

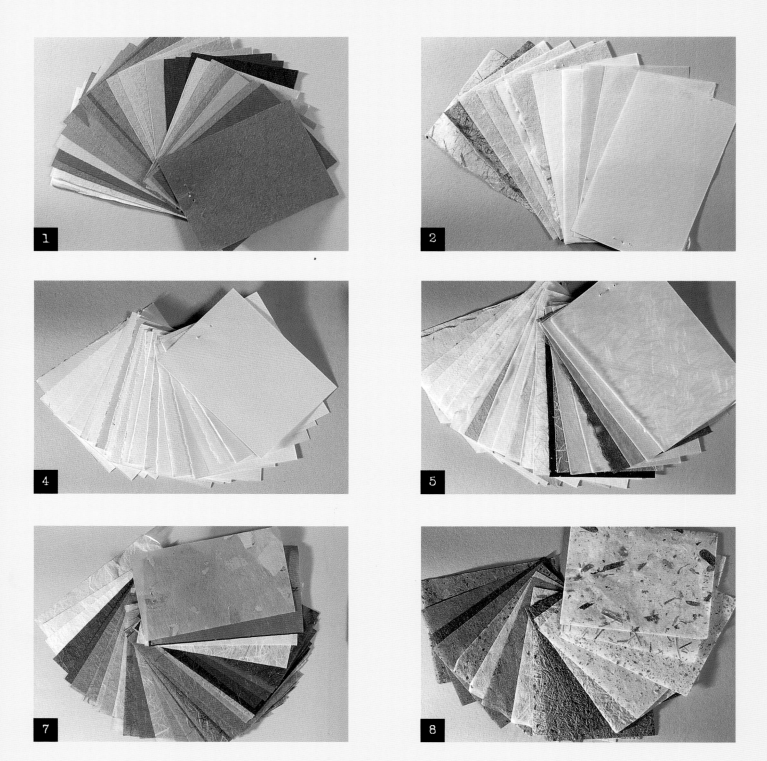

QUALITY PAPERS

1. *Moriki*

2. *Oriental specialty papers*

3. *Nepal and Bhutan handmades*

4. *Assorted bookweight and letterpress*

5. *Oriental specialty papers*

6. *Zerkall Ingres*

7. *Thailand Unryus*

8. *Thailand Chiri*

9. *Van Gelder*

Using Graphite with Specialty Papers

You can use the graphite method with many of these papers. Because the paper needs to be sprayed with water, however, some of the lightweight papers may fall apart when rubbed and the heavyweight ones may be too thick to pick up a refined image.

For fish rubbings, the lighter weight salago papers work well. Kozo and chiri papers are also good for this purpose. Thailand Chiri Unryu comes in many colors, and is available heavily or lightly speckled with gold or silver leaf.

There are many Japanese papers to experiment with. Hand papermaking is still practiced in many rural areas of Japan, although much imported paper is currently machine made. The range of Japanese paper is impressive; aside from its uses in the art field, it is used for making fans, lamps, screens, and many other commercial and decorative purposes.

Rice Paper

Perhaps because rubbing was first a Chinese art, using rice paper is traditional among rubbers. Rice paper is manufactured from the roots and leaves of the rice plant, which are soaked and cooked in large vats of water. A wire mesh frame is used to strain the suspension of macerated fibers. The frame and its fibers are put aside to dry in the form of matted sheets. Removed from the frame, the sheets of rice paper are then ready to be sold. Among the rice papers satisfactory for rubbing are Mulberry (both regular and student grades); Masa, smooth on one side; Kochi, opaque and extra heavy; and Troya. Although most of these papers sound as though they

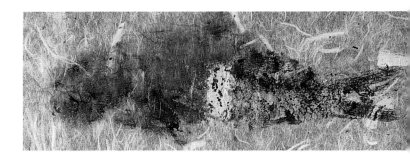

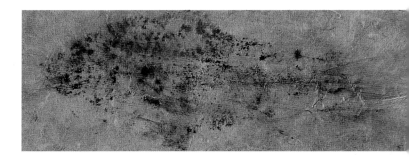

Different papers were used to make a fish print with varying degrees of success.

come from Japan, some are made here in the United States: Troya comes from Troy, New York!

Other Specialty Papers

Interesting effects can be achieved by using some of the more elegant and unusual oriental papers. Japanese Tea Chest paper comes in sheets of gold and silver, and can be used with various waxes to create attractive and distinctive rubbings. Fantasy Paper is also effective for rubbings. It comes in sheets 24 x 36 inches (60 x 90 cm) and has dried leaves and butterflies pressed into the layers of the paper. Wood veneer papers are also usable. Speedball puts out a printing paper that is satisfactory but a bit small.

People employed by cemeteries often use a paper called Blue Rubbing Paper to facilitate record keeping. It is actually a white paper with a purple tint, and is completely purple on the underside. This paper is taped to the stone and the surface is rubbed with a remnant of carpet. The design that emerges is light but clearly visible. This paper comes in rolls, and is available from cemetery-supply companies. It is a fragile paper, but it can be used to make a pictorial note of a subject you might later wish to use for a permanent rubbing.

There is an almost endless variety of papers. Just look around the larger art-supply stores. One handmade paper is called Nepal, the beautiful and traditional rubbing paper from the Orient. It is expensive. You can sometimes find other out-of-the-ordinary papers at reasonable prices; watch for sales and closeouts.

Cloth and Cloth-Backed Papers

Some "display" papers are actually cloth or cloth-backed and are adaptable for rubbing. Tracing cloth is strong; it has a white working side with a dull finish, and the back side is glazed. Sign cloth is also strong and has a smooth white surface. Smooth 100 percent cotton and silk yard goods can be used for rubbing. Fabrics that are 50 percent cotton and 50 percent polyester are also practical. A problem arises if you want to make the rubbings permanent, in which case the wax rubbing is set with a warm iron, and synthetic fabrics are not meant to withstand high temperatures. Certainly 100 percent synthetics are inappropriate for this purpose.

CRAYONS AND WAXES

You can obtain very interesting variations of the ordinary black-on-white rubbing by experimenting with different crayons, inks, and pigments. Most exotic is gold wax on black paper. You can also use colored tailor's chalks (available in notions stores), Cray-pas, ordinary primary crayons, lumber crayons, graphite sticks, or some of the imported English brass-rubbing supplies, such as Hardtmuth crayons or Astral heel balls. Lithographer's crayons or pencils are also good for rubbings. Some people have even tried rubbing with shoe polish and/or lipstick. I have also heard of using powdered charcoal mixed with beeswax.

Wax-based crayons can be used to best advantage when rubbing flat or incised surfaces. An extremely flat bas-relief can also be rubbed with waxes. English rubbing waxes are softer and, of course, more expensive than American gravestone rubbing waxes. Rubbing waxes come in many colors, including metallics, and are preferable to ordinary crayons because they are less likely to smear. I use fluorescent crayons when I want to do a multicolored design on the site.

English Heel Balls

English heel balls, often used for monumental brasses and gravestone rubbings, are made of wax and *lampblack*. (Lampblack is a finely powdered black soot collected from incompletely burned carbonaceous materials, and used as a pigment in painting, enamels, and printing inks.) Shoemaker's finishing wax is a good substitute for heel ball. It comes in two types, hard and soft, and is used in shoe-repair shops as a stain for covering scratches and scuffs on leather goods. This wax cake comes in a variety of shapes and under various brand names, but is available only in a limited number of colors. White, brown, and black may be available from local shoe-repair shops.

For those who wish to make their own rubbing wax, Henry Trivick suggests the following heel-ball recipe in his book *The Craft and Design of Monumental Brasses*:

Different effects can be achieved by adding colored waxes.

Russian tallow

Beeswax

Shellac: a natural resin, very hard but easily melted by heat

Household soap (very little)

Lampblack

The addition of shellac and lampblack in greater quantities will ensure a harder and blacker wax heel ball. The mixing quantities are largely a matter of experience. Slowly melt the tallow, the beeswax, and a little soap in a tin; then add the shellac and lampblack, and keep the mixture in a liquid form over low heat. Great care must be taken not to spill or let a flame near the composition. Mix well. When the mixture is thoroughly melted and mixed, pour it into preheated china egg cups, small coffee cups, or similar containers. Something slightly larger than the conventional egg cup makes an excellently shaped cake of rubbing wax suitable for large rubbings. For smaller pieces, pour the mixture into an open, two-ounce rectangular tobacco tin. When the mixture is cold, cut it into strips. Never use a plastic container—the hot wax will melt it—and never cool the wax composition quickly; the center will be the last part to cool off; as the composition shrinks, a hollow or split will develop in the middle.

Break large pieces of rubbing wax into smaller pieces to make it possible to lift fine detail from the subject you are rubbing. When you are on rubbing expeditions, carry your rubbing wax in your pocket or elsewhere on your person to keep it warm and ready for use, especially in cold weather.

Wax-Based Pencils

When working on small rubbings, especially those with fine details, wax-based colored pencils are very useful. Eagle brand Prismacolors are excellent, as are China marking pencils. Fossil rubbings are often done with these wax-based pencils. China markers wear down very rapidly: more than one pencil in a particular color would be needed for a large job.

PASTEL DYE STICKS

Pastel dye sticks are easy to use when you want to make a rubbing directly onto a piece of fabric. These sticks come in a variety of bright colors and are applied like crayons or rubbing wax. The colors do not become permanent until pressed through paper with a hot iron.

An advantage of this is that, if you are not pleased with your rubbing, you can, for the most part, wash it out. These dyes work best on cotton and silk fabrics. If you want the rubbing to be permanent, do not use 100 percent synthetic fibers, such as nylon, because these fibers cannot tolerate the temperatures of ironing.

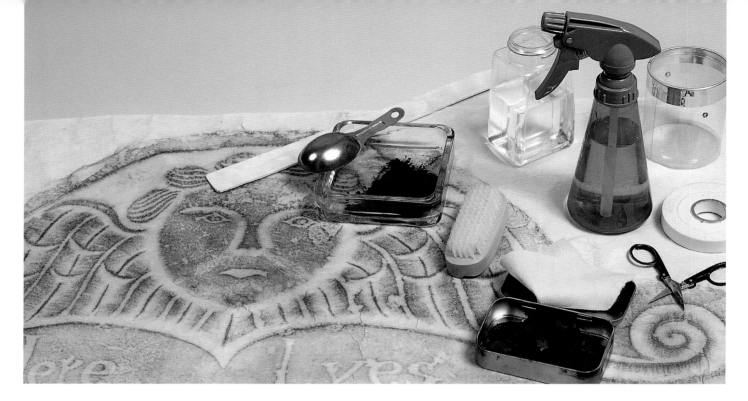

GRAPHITE

Graphite is a soft lustrous carbon used primarily for making so-called "lead" pencils, and as a basis for lubrication. Graphite is most often used for lifting rubbings when working on a raised surface (bas-relief). It is the easiest medium to master and can be used in place of inks or pigment mixtures.

Graphite is available in small tubes, as well as by the pound, from hardware stores and shops that make locks and keys. It is also available from chemical-supply houses and some art-supply stores. For our purposes, we used powdered graphite mixed with mineral oil. I suggest buying the powder in larger quantities; it becomes an expensive item when bought in tiny amounts. Graphite also comes in various stick and pencil forms that you can rub with or use to emphasize already rubbed designs. Graphite can also be purchased in paper sheets, similar to carbon paper.

You can make a graphite mixture for your rubbings by pouring a small amount of linseed oil into powdered (not flaked) graphite; any oil can be used, even cooking oil. Linseed oil, like some other oils, may tend to stain your paper with a yellowish tint, but it is hardly noticeable. A colorless oil like mineral oil may work the best. Use a small plastic or tin box to mix and store this mixture. The objective is to make a paste comparable in consistency to canned shoe polish. Slowly add small amounts of oil to the graphite and stir thoroughly. Experience will help you decide how thick a mixture you prefer to work with.

Work as neatly as possible. Graphite travels far! It is washable from most surfaces with soap and water or a scouring powder. When working with a graphite mixture, it is advisable to wear old clothing. The graphite comes out with washing or cleaning, but the oil residue may remain.

INKS

India inks, ink pads, paste inks, fountain pen ink, as well as all kinds of artists' inks, may be used for the wet technique. These might also include water-based printing inks, as well as oil-based ones. The ink is generally transferred to the paper by means of a dauber, or tamper, using a dabbing, rather than a rubbing stroke. Chinese renk ink or Sumi sticks are the traditional inks used since ancient times in the Orient.

The Japanese noun *Sumi* means carbon (charcoal) or black ink. This ink is called *India ink* in the States. The ink is produced from minute particles of carbon dust (soot) derived from the burning of plant parts, oil, and other materials. Glue or animal gelatin, and a preservative such as camphor, is added to the recipe. This mixture is then put into a mold to form it into a cube or cylinder and set aside to dry. To use the ink stick, you need to reconstitute the water. To accomplish this, simply rub the ink across a stone plate, after dipping it in a small amount of water. The stone plate is called a *suzuri* and has a small reservoir at the top to hold the ink.

Special Sumi inks without glue are available, but are difficult to find outside of Japan. These are specifically manufactured for stone rubbing and fish painting. (See Gyotaku on page 72.) Chaboku, a brownish variety of Sumi, is also available as is a blue/black type called Seiboku. Watercolors, preferably the kind in tubes, may be added to the Sumi ink to enhance the color.

Grinding your own ink is quite time-consuming. Commercially prepared liquid Sumi ink is avail-

This fish print was done with India ink on smooth cotton.

able and is both convenient and time saving, as it eliminates the need for grinding.

OTHER NECESSITIES

Aside from the materials discussed above, there are a number of other items you will find necessary when doing rubbings. Equip yourself with a good pair of scissors, one that can be used to cut paper, as well as to shear away obstructing grass and weeds. You should also have a fairly stiff brush to remove any grit or impurities from your subject. Never use a metal-bristle brush: it may scratch or damage the object you are cleaning. Use masking tape or freezer tape to tape your paper to the object you plan to rub. If you are working on very grainy stones, strapping tape will stick to them better. When practicing the wet technique you will need a sprayer. I use a fine-mist plant sprayer filled with water (if you're in the field, this should be carried in a plastic bag tied at the top).

Always carry a pencil so that you can write down the name of the site where your rubbing was completed. It is also wise to date it. Even when I am not on a rubbing expedition, I carry a small note pad in my purse, so that whenever I pass a good "rubbable," I note its characteristics and location so that I can return to the site at some future date. Without notes, it is almost impossible to remember where you saw what.

When you are doing a lengthy rubbing in what is often an uncomfortable position, you will find knee pads or a foam pad invaluable. On sunny days, wear a hat. Carry a small packet of disposable wipes for removing excess graphite or ink from your hands.

Carrying your work and supplies around is sometimes cumbersome. A mailing tube can serve as a carrier, but a map case with a built-in handle is handier and sturdier. You can punch a hole in each end of a mailing cylinder, however, and attach a cord; simply sling the tube over your shoulder. It is simple to carry your paper, rolled up in such a tube, both before and after your rubbing is complete. I prefer to carry all my supplies, the mailing tube as well, in a large, waterproof canvas bag. The bag I use is a machine-washable coal carrier. The only thing I don't put in the bag is rubbing wax, which as mentioned before, should be carried on your person to keep it warm enough for use. On a traveling vacation, the best way to carry your supplies is in a plastic shopping bag that you can attach to your body with a belt or hang from a backpack. If you need to fold the paper, you can press out the fold and wrinkles later with a warm steam iron.

Do not forget to obtain written permission, where necessary, to lift rubbings from public or private sites.

Rubbing from The Brass Rubbing Centre, London, England

DRY METHOD

The easiest rubbing technique is the dry method. A dry rubbing is accomplished by simply covering the surface to be rubbed with a piece of paper and rubbing the paper with a crayon. As simple as this sounds, it is still a good idea to experiment at home. Choose a few raised items (for example, coins, leaves, doilies, etc.) and cover them with ordinary paper. Trace over them with a soft pencil or crayon.

Right away you will probably see a few of the practical problems. For instance, it is necessary to have a suitable object to rub. The pencil may tear the paper. The crayon marking may overlap the design. The paper may move around. All these annoyances are easily overcome with practice. Once you are comfortable working with familiar objects, you will be ready to go out and search for new ones in the field.

FIRST FIELD TRIP RUBBING

For your first field trip, choose a rubbing site that interests you or one that is convenient to your home.

■ WHAT YOU NEED

Permission to lift a rubbing

Opaque but tough-quality good paper, preferably rice or hemp, in large sheets or rolls *or*

> Kraft paper (it's inexpensive and especially good for youngsters) *or*

> Heavy-weight tracing paper

Stiff brush (never use one with metallic bristles)

Scissors

Masking tape or freezer tape

Rubbing media (gravestone rubbing wax, heel ball, graphite, carpenter's crayon, etc.)

Large cylindrical tube for carrying paper and supplies

■ WHAT YOU DO

1. Be sure you have permission to lift a rubbing. Once you're at the site, look for an object with a clear, incised design. Choose a subject that is in good condition, not one with a severely eroded surface. In old cemeteries, brownstone markers are usually in better shape and easier to work from than markers of sandstone or other materials.

1

Riverside Cemetery, Asheville, North Carolina

2. Gently clean the surface with a stiff brush (never use a wire brush). If you're rubbing a gravestone, you might also wish to clip any long grass that might interfere with your work.

3. Cut the paper to size and tape it to the subject. On very grainy subjects, use strapping tape on top of the masking tape. Cover the object well so that if your rubbing medium slip, you won't mar the object.

4. Before you rub with wax, feel the design with your fingers. To begin the rubbing, lightly go over the entire surface with the wax to expose the raised portions (photo 1).

5. Next, broadly darken and begin to block out the complete design with the flat side of your crayon or wax (photos 2 and 3). If you desire, you can highlight certain areas with one or more differerent colors.

2

3

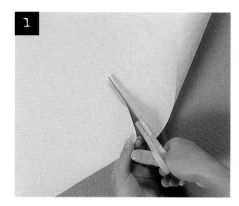

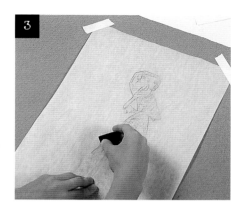

In the studio, we duplicated the essential steps of the dry rubbing technique using a brass facsimile.

WHAT YOU NEED

Object to rub that has a detailed, incised surface

Rubbing paper

Scissors

Masking tape

Wax crayons

Small piece of cardboard (optional)

Document repair tape

WHAT YOU DO

1. Cut the paper to size (photo 1).

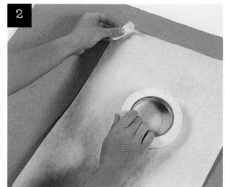

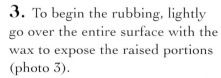

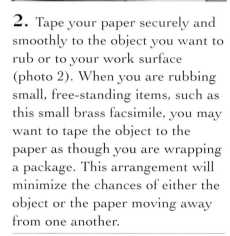

2. Tape your paper securely and smoothly to the object you want to rub or to your work surface (photo 2). When you are rubbing small, free-standing items, such as this small brass facsimile, you may want to tape the object to the paper as though you are wrapping a package. This arrangement will minimize the chances of either the object or the paper moving away from one another.

3. To begin the rubbing, lightly go over the entire surface with the wax to expose the raised portions (photo 3).

4. Next, broadly darken and begin to block out the complete design with the flat side of your crayon or wax (photo 4). Some people find it helpful to hold a small, flat piece of cardboard at

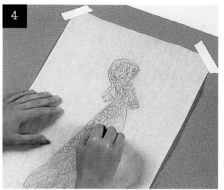

the edge of the design (feel with your fingers) so that out-of-bounds crayon strokes hit the cardboard instead of the paper. Following this blocking-in procedure, you'll see the design more clearly and be able to decide where you want the rubbing to appear darker or lighter.

5. Complete the rubbing by repeating the process where necessary with heavier pressure. If you are uncertain as to the breadth of the design, you can peek underneath the paper by loosening the tape at the bottom, making sure the rest of the piece is securely taped, and look under the paper. Replace the loosened tape and continue working. Never lift off the whole paper to see the surface underneath as it will be virtually impossible to exactly reposition the paper. When

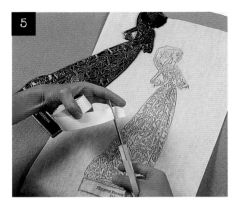

you are satisfied with the result, the rubbing is finished.

6. Gently peel the tape away from the paper. Any smears or unwanted lines may be removed from the paper with lighter fluid, cleaning fluid, or a rag soaked in paraffin. Just make certain to carry out this operation in a well-ventilated area.

7. As sometimes happens, the paper tore when I was rubbing this piece. What a great opportunity to demonstrate the use of document repair tape! Simply cut a piece of tape the size you need to adequately cover the tear (photo 5) and place the sticky, opaque tape on the back side of the rubbing. Use a flat stick to adhere it to the paper (photo 6). You will not be able to see the rip in the paper.

Margaret Bernard Peyton
1484

REVERSE RUBBING

Another variation is a resist process that produces a positive image from the subject, similar in concept to the positive in photography. In place of dark crayon on white paper, we use a light or colorless wax on white paper.

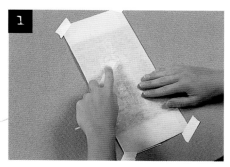

REVERSE RUBBING OF BRASS FACSIMILE

This technique is an extension of the dry technique described on page 63. The finished rubbing has a subtle, antiqued quality.

■ WHAT YOU NEED

Object to rub; detail should NOT be too fine

Hard-surfaced white paper (eg., English Brass rubbing paper or bond paper)

Masking tape

Hard, uncolored candle or colorless heel ball

Paper towels

Black India ink

Cellulose sponge

■ WHAT YOU DO

1. Tape the paper, securely to the subject.

2. Rub the paper with the colorless wax (photo 1). It will be difficult to see what you are doing but the sheen of the wax will become apparent if you look at it from an angle. Completely cover the subject with the wax, pressing hard.

3. Gently brush off any loose wax with a paper towel (photo 2).

4. Dampen the sponge with water. Dilute a small amount of India ink and test the color on a scrap of paper to make sure you are satisfied with the density of the ink. Then sponge the surface of the paper with ink (photo 3). Work quickly. As you rapidly cover the wax with the ink, the image of the rubbing will emerge (photo 4). Blot up any excess wetness with a paper towel.

An alternative to using India ink is to use a dark wood stain over the wax. This type of resist process is similar to the method used for making batik and it, too, needs to be carried out in a well-ventilated space.

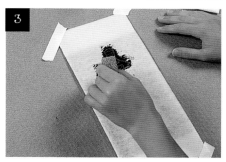

GRAPHITE METHOD

Another dry technique uses graphite mixed with mineral oil to form a paste. A recipe for graphite paste may be found on page 58. The completed rubbing using graphite looks quite different from the one made with wax; it has a softer, more gray look, as compared to the hard, dark edge of the wax picture.

MONUMENT RUBBED WITH WAX AND GRAPHITE

Although a wax media works best for rubbing an incised surface, graphite is more successful when the surface you are rubbing is somewhat raised. These two methods can also be combined, as was done with the handsome monument honoring Robert E. Lee, in Asheville, North Carolina. I prefer to use wax first and then go over it with graphite. If the detail of your subject is unclear, it sometimes helps to go over a wax rubbing with graphite while the paper is still taped to the object. This often helps to emphasize what is underneath.

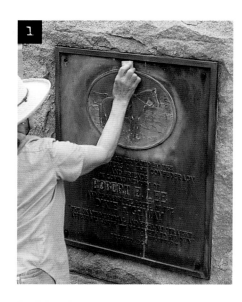

WHAT YOU NEED

Object to rub that has a detailed, incised surface

Rubbing paper

Stiff brush

Scissors

Masking tape

Spray bottle with water

Small piece of cardboard (optional)

Wax media

Graphite paste

Soft cloth or chamois

Paper towels

Disposable wipes

WHAT YOU DO

1. Clean the object well with the stiff brush (photo 1).

2. Cut the paper to size and tape it securely over the object you are rubbing (photo 2).

3. Lightly spray the paper with water. A light misting is all that is necessary (photo 3).

4. Wrap the cloth or chamois around your index finger and dip the cloth into the graphite paste; then wipe most of the graphite from this cloth onto another piece of cloth. The idea is to remove all impurities and clumps of graphite from your wrapped working finger. Excesses of graphite cause smearing and dark spots. With this technique, "less is more." You can always darken an area afterward, but the initial rubbing should be light.

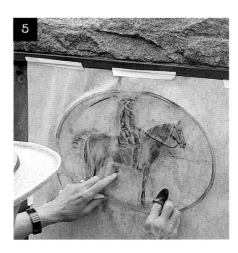

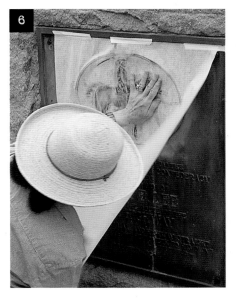

use cloth wrapped around several fingers: the work goes faster that way. You can make the design more like a drawing by going over, with more graphite, those places where you think shadows would emphasize its three-dimensionality. Some people call this method *dabbing* as they prefer to make a dabber of chamois. I believe this is unnecessary, and prefer to feel the surface underneath. If you find that you still pick up too much graphite on your cloth and your work looks smeary or too dark, wipe the rag's excess graphite onto paper toweling or newspaper before applying it to your paper.

6. If you loose track of the design, you can remove one taped corner and peek underneath (photo 6). Be sure to securely retape the paper.

7. Since working with graphite is somewhat messy, take along something to clean your hands with. When you return home, you can use soap, water, and a nail brush to completely remove the graphite.

8. Use the wax media to rub over the areas of the design you want to see in sharper, darker focus (photo 7).

9. The mineral oil in the graphite paste holds the graphite on the paper, so I have not found it necessary to use a fixative to prevent the finished rubbing from smearing. If you wish, however, you can further ensure the preservation of your work by coating it with a spray fixative.

5. Feel the design with one hand and spread the graphite with the other until you have rubbed the entire design (photos 4 and 5). For larger surfaces, you may prefer to

careful not to wet the paper too much or too little. You must also try to get a uniform amount of ink on the dabbers each time, and to remove any impurities that may collect on them.

PREPARING SUMI INK

Traditionally, Sumi ink stick is rendered into liquid by blending it with a small quantity of water on a *suzuri*, a smooth, hard stone with a small depression at one end. Some water is poured into this concavity and the Sumi stick is dipped into this water and then stroked back and forth on the flat surface of the stone plate. This process is repeated many times until the water turns a rich, dark, color. Sumi ink is also available in a cake form. For the project demonstrated on page 69, we used a liquid Sumi ink prepared commercially because it is the easiest to work with (refer to the source list on page 106).

You can make your own dabber by cutting a sponge into a small circle, scrunching it up, and covering it with a circular piece of soft fabric; 100 percent silk works best. Then bind the fabric around the sponge with a rubber band. When working with the ink and the dabber, be careful not to flood the dabber; the idea is to moisten it well.

If you wish to make your own wet kit to carry with you to a site, you can line the bottom of a covered plastic box with a sponge cut to fit snugly. Soak the sponge with Sumi ink.

WET METHOD

As your enthusiasm is sparked by the thought of all the interesting sites you can visit for the purpose of lifting rubbings, you might want to add the wet technique to your repertoire. It is also a dabbing process, and is most suited to uneven or deeply carved surfaces and medium-high bas-relief. This method for obtaining architectural details from buildings might, however, be frustrating for beginners since it is difficult to control.

A wet rubbing, broadly speaking, is made by attaching the paper to the object, dampening the paper, and tamping the paper-covered object with ink so as to produce a negative image on the paper. The resultant image appears softer and grayer (rather than blacker) than one produced by dry rubbing, but darker than one produced with graphite. Practice and patience is required to perfect the techniques of the wet method. You must be

METAL TRIVET RUBBED WITH INK

For this method, you can also use acrylic paints, block-printing inks, and dry pigments. If you use certain hemp papers, you may find that sticky paints will pick up the paper fiber and tear the paper.

■ WHAT YOU NEED

Rice or hemp paper

Stiff brush

Scissors

Masking tape

Fine-spray mister with water

Ink media (Sumi or water-based ink)

Dabber, about 1½ inches (4 cm) in diameter

Disposable wipes

■ WHAT YOU DO

1. Cut the paper to size and tape it to the object, although somewhat more loosely than with the dry method (photo 1).

2. Stand about 12 inches (10 cm) away from the paper, and use the sprayer to coat the paper with a fine mist of water (photo 2). Do not soak the paper, just moisten it. Let the paper dry for six to eight minutes. If necessary, retape the paper to get a more uniform fit and to smooth out any wrinkles and/or air bubbles.

3. Gently but firmly mold the paper with your fingertips to the object's surface (photo 3). Loosen the tape and paper further if they are still too taut.

4. When the paper is *almost* dry, wet the dabber in the ink and blot the dabber on the paper towel so that it is moist, but not soaked (photo 4).

5. Dab the surface of the rubbing paper; do not rub or stroke it (photo 5 on page 70). Give the ink time to be absorbed by the paper. If the paper should appear dry in certain spots, remoisten it with a paper towel or spray it lightly; the ink will not run. Continue with the dabbing procedure until you are satisfied with the results. Practice is required to get the feel of this technique. Experience will tell you how much ink to apply and how wet the paper should be.

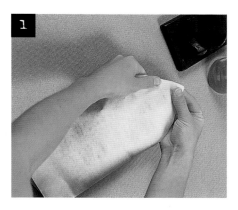

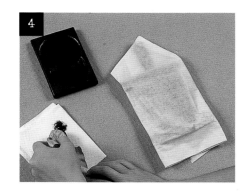

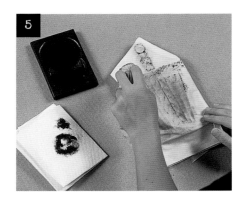

6. When you are finished, remove the tape and paper from the object. If you are working at a site, allow the paper to dry completely; then roll it up and place it in the cylinder. When you arrive home, place the rubbing between two large sheets of clean paper. Weigh it down with books and allow it to completely flatten.

A More Challenging Approach

A more complicated wet technique can be used if you are rubbing stone with inks that contain little or no water. Described by John Bodor in his book, *Rubbing and Textures*, the stone object is moistened with a combination of methyl cellulose and water. This simultaneously causes the paper to adhere to the stone and to dampen it. Then, after the paper dries and before the ink is used, Bodor recommends brushing the surface of the paper with beeswax, which prevents the ink from penetrating the paper. At this point one proceeds, as above, with the ink-dabbing process.

USING GRAPHITE PASTE FOR WET RUBBINGS

My own preference in wet methods is one which employs an oil-and-powdered graphite paste, the same mixture described on page 58. The difference here is that, before applying the graphite paste, you spray the hemp paper with water until it is quite damp.

WOODEN MEDALLION RUBBED WITH GRAPHITE

Using graphite paste on dampened paper gives this rubbing the look of a charcoal drawing. This is one of my favorite ways to lift a rubbing.

■ WHAT YOU NEED

Object to rub that has a detailed, incised surface

Hemp paper

Scissors

Masking tape

Small piece of cardboard (optional)

Spray bottle with water

Graphite paste

Soft cloth or chamois

Paper towels

Disposable wipes

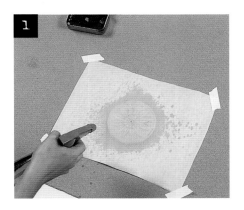

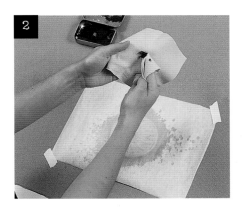

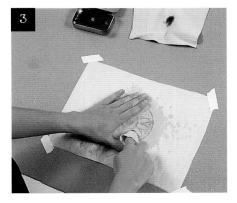

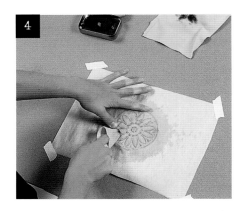

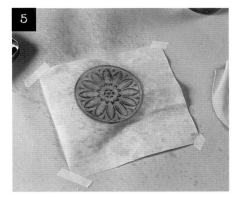

▨ WHAT YOU DO

1. Cut the paper to size and tape it over the object.

2. Spray the paper so that it is thoroughly damp (photo 1). You should be able to see the design under the wet paper.

3. Wrap the cloth or chamois around your index finger and dip the cloth into the graphite paste. Wipe most of the graphite from this cloth onto another piece of cloth (photo 2).

4. As you apply the graphite paste, mold the wet paper to the surface you are rubbing (photos 3 and 4). This technique is especially good for somewhat higher

reliefs, and I find it easier to control than the ink version of the wet method. You are less likely to get results that are too dark or smeary in certain areas.

5. Photo 5 shows the finished rubbing. Photo 6 shows (on the left) a rubbing done with Sumi ink and (on the right) a rubbing made with graphite paste. Both are attractive. As you work with different materials and methods, you will find the ones that you prefer, in part based on the types of objects you are rubbing and the kind of results you want to achieve.

FISH PRINTING (Gyotaku)

Gyotaku is a Japanese noun. The Chinese calligraphic character is fish and the phonetic sound is "gyo." The other character means "stone monument rubbing" and that is phonetically pronounced "taku."

A fish rubbing, accomplished with wet paper and ink, is also an excellent example of what is known as the *direct method* of rubbing. This approach would be considered destructive on any surface other than a fish, flower, or leaf because it requires that the object itself be covered with ink and the paper then pressed to that surface. This method works well on paper and fabric.

Traditionally in Japan, a fish rubbing, sometimes called *fish printing*, is used to record the specifications of fish caught by game fishermen. Some contests even use a gyotaku as the entry certificate for the fish caught.

FISH PRINT WITH THE DIRECT METHOD

▮ WHAT YOU NEED

Whole fish, with scales on and innards left in; deep sea fish, such as grouper or red snapper, work well

Sheet of cardboard

Liquid detergent

Paper towels

Corrugated cardboard

Small straight pins

Sumi ink, concentrated watercolor, or tempera paint

Strong Japanese rice paper, 100 percent lightweight cotton cloth, or 100 percent silk

Paintbrush, about 1 inch (2.5 cm) wide

Craft knife

Disposable wipes

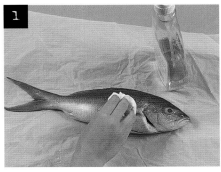

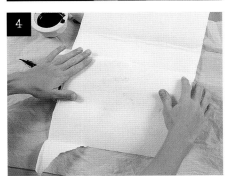

WHAT YOU DO

1. Cover your work surface with a sheet of cardboard. Place the fish on a piece of scrap paper. Clean the fish with liquid detergent to remove the mucous film from its surface, as well as other excretions from various orifices (photo 1). This is an important procedure because these excretions impart a stickiness to the ink, which interferes with its application, and to the paper, which makes it difficult to remove when you are finished with the print.

2. Use small blocks of corrugated cardboard or rolled up paper towels to prop up parts of the fish so that more of the surface area of the fish will be in contact with the paper (photo 2). Fan out the fins. A small amount of cotton or tissue may be stuffed into the mouth if you wish to retain an open position.

3. Brush over the entire fish with the medium of your choice, covering it with strokes going in one direction (photo 3). Go back over any areas of the fish that have dried.

4. Blot the fish lightly with a paper towel (photo 4).

5. Center the rice paper or fabric on top of the fish; do not attempt to reposition it or you will wind up with a smeared print. You can always trim the paper or fabric later or cover the printed image with a mat to make it appear cen-

tered. Starting at the center of the fish, smooth the material against the surface of the fish (photo 5). Work out from the center, molding the paper to the contour of the fish. Be careful not to let the paper shift or the print will be blurred. Rub the surface of the paper gently. You will be able to see the fish print begin to show through the paper (photo 6). Press gently around the fins, gills, and the mouth, and make sure that outline of the fish is visible.

6. Carefully remove the paper.

7. Allow the rubbing to dry. If there are too many wrinkles in the paper to suit your taste, you may iron the paper. I recommend that you cover the ironing board with a clean sheet of paper and place another piece between the rubbing and the iron.

R U B B I N G   O N   F A B R I C

You can create very attractive rubbings on fabric. I am particularly fond of making rubbings of items from nature, such as dried leaves, ferns, seashells, and even coral. The method is basically the same as the dry method using paper.

S E L E C T I N G   A N D   P R E P A R I N G   T H E   F A B R I C

Selecting the correct fabric is important; the smoother the fabric, the easier it is to lift a quality rubbing. Lightweight, 100 percent cotton, the kind used for bed sheets or men's shirting, is ideal. Chinese silk works extremely well. Avoid fabrics such as nylon that are 100 percent synthetic; they are not made to withstand the temperatures of ironing that you use to set the wax media. A heavier fabric, such as linen, does not pick up the rubbing the same way as silk or cotton, but the rubbing has an attractive look.

It is a good idea to experiment on a scrap of the fabric you choose to make sure you will be satisfied with the results.

Prepare the fabric by washing it and removing the sizing, this ensures that the wax media will be absorbed and not wash out. Dry the material and iron it to produce a smooth surface.

T Y P E S   O F   W A X   M E D I A

There are several varieties of crayon from which to choose. Waterproof lumber crayons, manufactured by Binney and Smith, are simple to use. The crayons are available in eight colors. They are especially good for children to use because they are firm and do not smear easily. Lumber crayons are best for

transferring rubbings of leaves and relatively flat or incised surfaces. They produce a clear, sharp line.

An alternative to lumber crayons are ordinary coloring crayons. The main advantages of these crayons are that they come is many colors, can be blended, and are widely available. In addition, regular crayons are softer than lumber crayons, which means that the rubbed image is not as sharp, which gives a different effect that may be desirable.

Pastel dye sticks or dyeing pastels, as they are sometimes called, require more skill to use. They are very soft and tend to smear if your fingers linger on them. You need to work with them very gingerly to avoid contact with what you have already rubbed. Their redeeming feature is that you can lift shallow bas-relief, as well as flat objects. After setting the color with an iron, there may be some wax bleeding around the image. This is not an unpleasant effect. If you do not like the design, do not iron it; wash the fabric immediately.

RUBBING TECHNIQUE

If you are rubbing a small object, simply hold the fabric taut against the object with one hand, and, with the other hand, rub the fabric with the crayon, moving the crayon only in one direction. A variation of this method is to place the object to be rubbed on a piece of cardboard, stretch the fabric over the object, and pin it in place. Then rub the fabric with the crayon, again being sure to rub only in one direction.

SETTING THE COLORS

To set the colors and make them permanent, you need to iron the rubbed fabric. First, cover your ironing board with a piece of blank paper large enough to accommodate the wax design. Place the rubbing, face down, on the fabric, and cover it with a few sheets of blank paper to protect both the fabric and the iron. Press over the paper-covered fabric with a hot iron. When you lift the paper, you will see the wax residue on the paper.

USING A LIGHT BOX

I have devised a somewhat more complicated procedure for rubbing on fabric, but the resultant image is improved and worth the extra steps. I glue the items to be rubbed onto small sheets of clear acrylic with a neutral pH adhesive, such as Elmer's or Sobo glue. Then I place the acrylic sheets on a light box and tape the fabric to the box with masking tape. When I switch on the light, the objects I want to rub are visible through the fabric, and it is much easier to accomplish detailed rubbings. I am also able to move the acrylic sheets to different positions under the fabric or add additional sheets to create the finished design. Another approach would be to tape the acrylic sheets to a window and take advantage of natural light.

SILK RUBBING WITH GINGKO LEAVES

I like the effect you can achieve with these lovely leaves, but other dried materials work well, too. The key is to rub slowly and carefully so that you do not rip the fragile materials.

■ WHAT YOU NEED

China silk or other smooth fabric (avoid synthetics)

Dried leaves, small ferns, or pressed flowers

Masking tape

White glue

Sheet of clear plastic

Light box (optional)

Crayons

Pastel dye sticks

Iron and ironing board

Large sheets of blank paper

■ WHAT YOU DO

1. Glue the dried leaves onto the plastic sheet and place it on a light box (photo 1).

2. Tape the silk to the light box so that it will not shift while you are rubbing (photo 2).

3. Use crayons and pastel dye sticks to rub over the outline of the leaves (photo 3). Remember to rub in one direction only.

4. Use contrasting colors of your wax media to fill in details and shading (photo 4).

5. Cover your ironing board with scrap paper. Place the silk on the paper, with the rubbed images face down. Then cover the silk with another piece of paper, and iron the silk (photo 5). Ironing in this way seals the wax to the fabric and removes any excess.

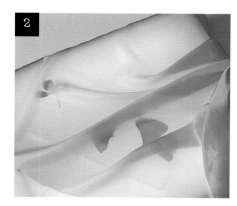

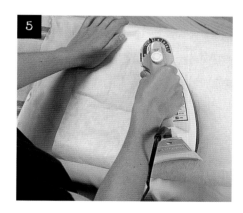

EMBELLISHED BED LINEN

You can also add appealing accent motifs to fabric by rubbing a length of lace that has a lot of interesting surface texture and detail.

■ WHAT YOU NEED

Cotton bed sheets

Lace border or trim

Spray adhesive

Masking tape

Pastel dye sticks or crayons

Iron and ironing board

Large sheets of blank paper

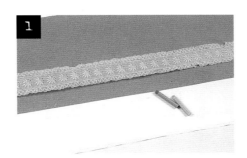

■ WHAT YOU DO

1. Spray the back of the lace with a light coating of spray adhesive and adhere the lace to a piece of paper on your work surface (photo 1).

2. Position the area of the sheet you want to rub on top of the lace and tape the sheet securely (photo 2).

3. Use the wax media to rub over the lace (photo 2).

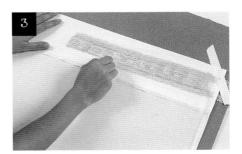

4. If you like, you can go back over the design using a contrasting color (photo 3).

HERE LIES
YE GRAVESTONE ARTWEAR™ COLLECTION

GRAVESTONE ARTWEAR™ OF YORK VILLAGE, MAINE, PRODUCES T-SHIRTS, PURSES, SCARFS, WALL CALENDARS, RUBBER STAMPS, AND OTHER ITEMS BEARING STRIKING DESIGNS FROM ANCIENT HEADSTONES. THROUGH CAREFUL RUBBING ON SPECIAL PAPER, THE SHOP HAS PRESERVED HUNDREDS OF IMAGES REPRESENTING THE EVOLUTION OF GRAVESTONE CARVING IN NEW ENGLAND, INCLUDING SEVERAL CELTIC DESIGNS. THE MOTIFS RANGE FROM PRIMITIVE 17TH-CENTURY SYMBOLS TO MORE SOPHISTICATED AND ARTISTIC TABLEAUX OF THE 19TH CENTURY.

OWNERS PAULETTE CHERNACK AND HER DAUGHTER CASSANDRA CHERNACK SEEK OUT GRAVESTONES TO RUB; THEN SILKSCREENS ARE MADE, WHICH ARE USED TO APPLY THE RICHLY DETAILED ART WORKS TO CLOTHING, SOAP, NOTE CARDS, AND MORE. THE RESULT IS A DISTINCTIVE COMBINATION OF CHARM AND HIP, OTHERWORLDLY FLAIR. FOR INFORMATION, REFER TO THE MAIL-ORDER LIST ON PAGE 106.

I have hundreds of rubbings. My personal storage method consists of simply rolling up the rubbings and slipping them into enormous wicker baskets. I do label the outside of the rubbings, however, or I'd never locate anything. A better system is to roll each rubbing into a cardboard cylinder and label the cylinder.

FLAT STORAGE

Rubbings, especially smaller ones, may also be stored flat. I have seen beautiful bound folios constructed to contain a series of rubbings. A particularly impressive set I have seen is a limited edition series of early American gravestone rubbings produced by Ann Parker and Avon Neal. On this page you will see a rubbing from another of their limited edition series. In any event, flat storage can be accomplished with corrugated cardboard or just by placing the rubbings in flat files or any other flat boxes or drawers. Just make certain to label everything with date, location, and any other pertinent facts.

IRONING YOUR RUBBINGS

No matter which storage method you choose, remember that it is possible and usually desirable to iron your rubbings to flatten them out before you frame them. Do protect both your ironing board and iron by placing sheets of newspaper, covered with a sheet of blank paper, between the rubbing and the iron and between the ironing board cover and the rubbing. It is safe to use a steam iron; be sure to keep the heat setting on low, especially when you are ironing rubbings made with wax crayons. It is a good idea to first experiment with the temperature of the iron on a dispensable rubbing.

WAYS TO FRAME RUBBINGS

Rubbings look wonderful framed. You can create very attractive decorative elements for your home by choosing interesting frames. Small rubbings, of a uniform size, can be framed in matching frames and hung on the wall as a series.

The most conventional way to display the rubbings is to mat and frame them as you would any work on paper. The problems begin when the work is larger than the standard sizes for mat board, glass, or plastic covering. Once you exceed the standard measurements, everything becomes more costly. Aside from larger sheets of glass or plastic, you must purchase a sturdier frame to accommodate the heavier weight. Glare-free glass also adds to the price. If you only have a single rubbing to frame, or several smaller ones that you want in identical frames

to coordinate with your decor, you may want to frame them yourself.

Shrink Wrap

Shrink wrap, also called *museum mount*, is a relatively inexpensive alternative for both displaying and preserving your rubbings. Basically it is a process similar to the way meat is wrapped in the supermarket. The rubbing is placed on a foam board, which in turn is covered with clear plastic wrap. The plastic is then heat sealed from the back of the board, and a hanger apparatus is attached. A very big advantage of this format is that the result, aside from being attractive, is extremely lightweight and airtight. Some commercial packaging firms will give you a cheaper price if you have a quantity of work all in one size.

Dry Mount

Another, relatively inexpensive, but attractive, means of displaying your rubbings is with *dry mount*, a process through which a print is bonded to cardboard using a particular heat-sensitive tissue. Framers often prepare work for dry mount, but it is more likely that you will find a fully equipped studio by seeking a specialist in photo mounting. Rubbings can also be dry mounted onto cloth.

Positionable dry mounting adhesive is a product that makes dry mounting easier, if you want to try it yourself. I doubt that it will look as elegant as a professional's finished work, but it will be less expensive. The adhesive transfers to the reverse of the rubbing to be mounted; you place the rubbing face-up on the adhesive sheet and then lift it up. The adhesive transfers to the back of the rubbing, ready to be adhered to the cardboard. A permanent bond is formed, when the adhesive is burnished into position. (Burnishers, for this purpose, are sold where you purchase the adhesive.) It is also possible to detach the so-called permanent bond with rubber cement solvent.

Museum-Quality Results

It is easy to mount your rubbings onto sheets of museum-quality mat board with archival linen tape or archival glues. The mat around the rubbing should be of the same quality mat board. This is a good, simple approach.

You can purchase an inexpensive hanger just for rubbings made of two strips of grooved plastic (see the source list on page 106). You simply slip the top and bottom of the rubbing into each of the two strips. The upper section has string attached for hanging.

PRAGMATIC USES FOR RUBBINGS

Rubbings are employed for many practical purposes. Archaeologists use rubbings when photography is impractical. For example, the interiors of vases are not always visible to the naked eye, but an inked dabber on a long stick can be used in conjunction with rolled up rubbing paper to "print" the inside textures. Museums also make use of rubbings: when something is not clearly visible they will "bring up" the design by rubbing.

Dealers and collectors of antiquities, such as Japanese Tsuba (sword guards), for example, will often trade rubbings of items from their collections to each other to display their wares or convey their needs. Much buying and selling is done in this manner.

Recording Petroglyphs

Scholars in many fields illustrate their findings with rubbings. American Indian petroglyphs from rocks or cave walls are well suited to the process; however, these petroglyphs are considered endangered, as they are part of this ancient culture, serving both magical and religious purposes. Currently, Indians do use the rubbings, which they "lift" onto animal hides during certain healing ceremonies, but they require special permission to enter protected areas to obtain them.

Here is a photograph of a Taino petroglyph from Puerto Rico. These petroglyph designs represent zoomorphic, anthropomorphic, as well as abstract forms.

Recently I came across a book on English medieval graffiti in which the author lifted rubbings with a hard pencil from church walls and pillars within a 60-mile radius of Cambridge.

Household Applications

More ordinary uses for rubbings might simply be to get a clearer impression of the metallic manufacturer's label on an old piece of furniture or of the hallmarks on a piece of silver. To shop for a matching pattern for your flatware, just make a rubbing of it. You can do the same thing to replace an embossed floor tile. If a beloved pet has died, and you had a headstone installed to mark where it was buried, you could do a rub-

bing of the stone. This one from a pet cemetery is quite charming and would be sweet framed.

Reproducing Rubbings

Rubbings reproduce well. They can be used as illustrations for stationery, bookplates, newsletters, calendars, and brochures, especially those relating to community or charitable projects. A group in Brooklyn, New York, illustrated a

fund-raising cookbook with rubbings of local landmarks to accompany their provincial recipes. A church made prints of the rubbings lifted from the mason's boasting pattern, and sold them to raise needed funds. Another church made a large poster of the Lamb of God lifted from the Pilgrim's Pavement in the cathedral, and sold it. A synagogue illustrated its walking tour handbook with rubbings from its landmark building.

Craft Projects

Craft magazines, books, and shops are infinite sources of inspiration for projects you can create or adapt from your rubbings. If you think you've ruined a rubbing, you can use it to make an unusual kite or distinctive wrapping paper. In fact, once I received a present wrapped in an inexpensive Siamese rubbing; I assure you I did not discard the wrapper.

The following chapter features a dozen creative and attractive projects that use a completed rubbing or a rubbing as the basis for a design. Once you turn your attention to rubbings, I am sure you will dream up dozens of other ways to use your rubbings.

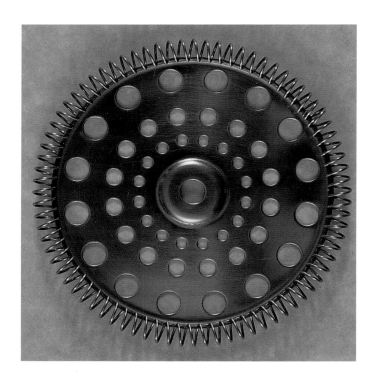

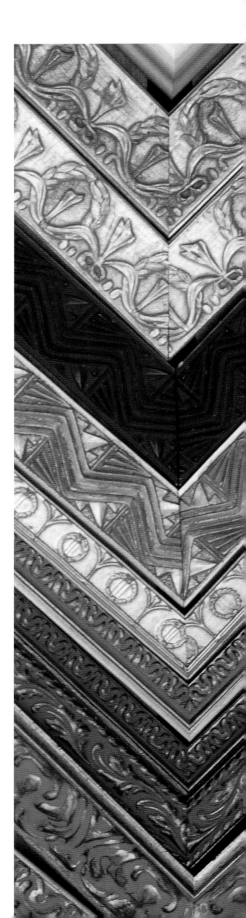

NOTE CARDS

It is very simple to make your own note cards. For this project I visited the Waldorf Astoria Hotel in New York City. I did many rubbings throughout the building, but the very small rubbings I did of the doorknobs seemed most appropriate to use in making individual note cards.

■ WHAT YOU NEED

One or several rubbings on paper

Construction paper
or other card stock

Blank note cards prepared
commercially (optional)

Envelopes

Neutral pH adhesive or white glue

Scissors

Ribbon

Metallic pens

Beads or other accessories

*Note: If you use a commercial
printer, it is possible to use any
rubbing as these printers are able
to reduce the rubbing to the
desired size.

Designer: Terry Taylor

■ WHAT YOU DO

1. Fold the card stock paper in half. Measure the card paper to the size envelope you intend to use.

2. Cut the rubbing to an appropriate size to look attractive on the paper stock you have selected.

3. Glue the rubbing onto the paper with white glue or pH neutral adhesive. Leave a border around the image. Generally the border should be larger at the bottom than on the other three sides.

4. Embellish the cards with ribbons, beads, or drawn-on details.

(continued on page 86)

(continued from page 85)

USING A COMMERCIAL PRINTER

I had a series of rubbings printed for me by a commercial printer (shown on page 81 and below). Then I packaged them and sold them to museum shops. Among the selections I offered were an Art Deco series, botanicals, and Judaica. When ordering from a printer, there is always a minimum number of pieces you must order—generally, 500 of each design. You could try to make cards with your own computer, too.

Left: Ark doors, Central Synagogue, New York City

Below: Art Deco detail, Bronx Courthouse, New York

CELEBRITY FEUD

IT IS INTERESTING TO NOTE THAT THE EMPIRE STATE BUILDING STANDS ON THE ORIGINAL SITE OF THE WALDORF ASTORIA HOTEL. IN THE EARLY 1890S, A BROUHAHA DEVELOPED BETWEEN MRS. WILLIAM ASTOR AND HER NEPHEW WILLIAM WALDORF ASTOR, WHO OWNED THE HOUSE ACROSS THE GARDEN AT 33RD AND FIFTH. THE NEPHEW CONSTRUCTED A 13-STORY HOTEL (THE WALDORF HOTEL) ON HIS PROPERTY AS AN ACT OF VENGEANCE; HIS WIFE, IT SEEMS, HAD BEEN UNSUCCESSFUL IN WRESTING THE LEADERSHIP TITLE OF NEW YORK SOCIETY GRANDE DAME FROM "AUNTIE." THE WALDORF OPENED ON MARCH 14, 1893. MRS. ASTOR GAVE UP THE BATTLE, FINALLY, AND MOVED UPTOWN. ON NOVEMBER 1, 1897 A CONNECTING HOTEL, THE ASTORIA, WAS BUILT ON THE SITE OF HER FORMER PROPERTY. THIS FIRST HOTEL CLOSED IN 1929 PRIOR TO THE STOCK MARKET CRASH. THE RIGHTS TO THE NAME OF THE HOTEL WERE RETAINED. THE WALDORF ASTORIA REOPENED IN 1931 AT ITS PRESENT LOCATION.

Designer: Heather Smith

Gift Wrapping Paper

With a little help from a grown-up, children can make festive wrapping paper by rubbing shells, coins, leaves, and other objects, using ordinary tissue paper and crayons.

■ WHAT YOU NEED

Tissue paper

Objects to rub

Double-sided tape

Wax crayons

■ WHAT YOU DO

1. Position the tissue paper over the object to be rubbed. You may want to help the child put a piece of double-sided tape on the bottom of the object to be rubbed; then secure the taped object to the work surface so it will not move when the child is rubbing it.

2. Use crayons to make a rubbing of the object. Repeat the motif all over the paper. Use other objects to create a pleasing design.

(continued on page 88)

Gift Paper and Frame

(continued from page 87)

Frugal Frame

A child can also make this simple frame with some of the completed tissue paper (and a little help from grown-up hands). This would be an especially great gift for grandparents or for a favorite teacher who has accumulated one too many apples.

■ WHAT YOU NEED

Corrugated cardboard
(a box with flaps works best)

Ruler

Pencil

Craft knife or scissors

Craft glue

Paper or fabric rubbings

Drawing or photograph

■ WHAT YOU DO

1. Measure and cut a piece of cardboard to the size and shape you desire for your frame. Be creative: picture frames are fascinating when shaped as octagons or triangles. For a free-standing frame (as shown here), leave one of the box flaps attached to use as a support.

2. Center a drawing or photograph on the front of the cardboard and trace along the outer edges. Using this outline as a guide, draw a smaller rectangle (or other shape) for the inside edge of the frame.

3. Use a craft knife to cut out the center piece. You should now have a basic frame ready for decorating.

4. Make a rubbing on tissue paper, as described above.

5. Cut the paper in strips large enough to cover each length of the frame. Wrap the strips around the edges. Lay the strips on top of the frame to check for proper coverage and placement.

6. Working in sections, smooth craft glue in a thin layer along the surface of the cardboard with your fingertip. Press the decorated strips of paper or fabric to the gluey frame (there should be extra width and length on each strip to cover the edges). Wrap and glue the extra material to cover the inside and outside edges of the frame.

7. Decorate the back of the frame in the same manner.

8. Use a little tape on the back of the frame to hold the drawing or photograph in place.

Rubbing paper

Permission letter for rubbing at the site

Rubbing paper

Materials for making a dry rubbing (wax)

Completed round rubbing

Scissors

Glass top of equal size of table and rubbing

Round tablecloth in color that complements the rubbing

WHAT YOU DO

1. Trim the rubbing to fit the round table.

2. Cover the table with the cloth. Place the rubbing on top and cover it with the glass.

Note: You can also do the rubbing directly onto the fabric using pastel dye sticks. See page 75 for details. Many pattern companies offer patterns for sewing round tablecloths.

This attractive tablecloth topper is made with a rubbing I lifted from a manhole cover in Madrid, Spain. Not all cities have such beautiful ones!

I must admit that I did not try to get permission to do this rubbing, as I thought it would be a major production. The major production occurred, however, when a police officer was ready to arrest me for "trying to poison the water of Madrid." It was not easy to explain, in English, that I just wanted to do a rubbing. Fortunately I had a copy of my first book on rubbing, with my picture on the cover. The message got through, but I did not push my luck: I did not do any additional rubbings at that site.

This is a simple way to make attractive bookmarks. I used decorative note papers, but you can make the bookmarks with any type of fancy paper.

■ WHAT YOU NEED

Object to rub

White paper

Crayons

Decorative paper

White glue

Scissors

Hole punch

Gold cord or colored ribbon

■ WHAT YOU DO

1. Make the rubbing on good-quality white paper.

2. Cut the decorative paper into strips the size of bookmarks.

3. Trim the rubbing so it will fit on the decorative paper.

4. Glue the rubbing onto the decorative paper.

5. Punch holes in one end of the bookmark and slip in a length of gold cord or ribbon. Tie the two ends of the cord or ribbon to make a loop.

For this screen, I lifted three rubbings of the elevator doors in the Woolworth Building in New York City. I knew I needed a motif that would be large enough and dramatic enough to work with the scale of a room divider. I think the results are spectacular.

■ WHAT YOU NEED

Permission letter for rubbing at site

Large roll of rubbing paper

Colored rubbing wax in colors of your choice

Masking tape

Scissors

Mending tissue

Tape measure

Stepladder

Screen in need of refurbishing

Paint

Paintbrushes

Craft knife

Rubber cement

■ WHAT YOU DO

Making the Rubbing

1. Make three rubbings using the dry technique as described on page 63.

(continued on page 92)

Room Divider

(continued from page 90)

Covering the Screen

1. We were very lucky with this one! When I was in Asheville for the photo shoot for this book, my editor and I visited one of that city's terrific antique malls where we found this room divider. It was not expensive; two of the three rice paper panels were torn, but otherwise the screen was in great shape. Look for screens at rummage sales, yard sales, and antique stores. You might be in luck, too!

2. Paint the wooden frame a color that works well with your home decor. Let the frame dry.

3. Measure the size of the openings in the screen. Carefully cut the rubbings to fit inside each panel.

4. Coat one of the paper panels in the screen and the back of one of the rubbings with rubber cement. Adhere the rubbing to the paper panel and smooth it flat.

5. Repeat this procedure with the other two panels and rubbings.

FRANK W. WOOLWORTH, A FARM BOY FROM UTICA, NEW YORK, BUILT FOR HIMSELF A "CATHEDRAL OF COMMERCE." FOR NEARLY 20 YEARS, IT WAS THE WORLD'S TALLEST BUILDING. THE WOOLWORTH BUILDING, LOCATED IN DOWNTOWN MANHATTAN, COST $13,500,000 WHEN IT WAS BUILT IN 1913 AND WAS PAID FOR COMPLETELY IN CASH. THE ARCHITECT WAS CASS GILBERT, WHO EXPLAINED THAT THE INTERIOR OF THE BUILDING WAS INFLUENCED BY "15TH CENTURY GOTHIC."

THE FIRST THING I NEEDED TO DO WAS OBTAIN PERMISSION FOR MY HUSBAND AND MYSELF TO LIFT RUBBINGS FROM THE ELEVATOR DOORS AND THEIR SURROUNDING BORDERS. THIS ACCOMPLISHED, WE MEASURED THE DOORS AND CUT PAPER TO FIT, LEAVING ENOUGH SPACE ALL AROUND FOR TAPING THE PAPER. WE TRIED TO LEAVE THE PAPER SOMEWHAT LOOSE IN THE CORNERS SO IT WOULD NOT TEAR. WE MADE FOUR RUBBINGS OF THE PANELS; THE EXTRA ONE WAS FOR "JUST IN CASE." (IN FACT, THE PAPER DID RIP A FEW TIMES AND WE REPAIRED THESE TEARS AT HOME WITH TISSUE MENDING PAPER, AS DESCRIBED ON PAGE 64.) THE DOORS WERE VERY HIGH, SO IT WAS NECESSARY TO MOUNT A SMALL STEPLADDER TO BE ABLE TO REACH THE TOPS.

FIRST WE WENT OVER THE PAPER WITH A RUST-COLORED WAX. WHEN THE DESIGN WAS VISIBLE, WE WENT OVER IT AGAIN TO DARKEN IT. THEN WE RUBBED THE IMAGE IN A DELIBERATELY HAPHAZARD MANNER WITH AN ORANGE WAX TO GIVE THE DESIGN AN AGED APPEARANCE. FINALLY, WE RUBBED IN THIS WAY AGAIN WITH BLUE WAX.

THOMAS WOLFE ANGEL

YOU CAN ACHIEVE TERRIFIC RESULTS BY RUB-
BING ON DARK PAPER USING LIGHT-COLORED
WAX OR CRAYONS. METALLIC GOLD AND
SILVER SHOW UP ESPECIALLY WELL.

THE PHOTO HERE SHOWS ME RUBBING
A SIDEWALK MARKER IN ASHEVILLE, NORTH
CAROLINA, COMMEMORATING THE WRITER
THOMAS WOLFE, WHO GREW UP IN THAT
CITY. I AM USING JUST WHITE WAX. AS
YOU CAN SEE, HIS FAMOUS ANGEL EMERGES
FROM THE BLACK PAPER, AS IF BY MAGIC!

DECORATIVE WINDOW TREATMENTS

For this project I visited an Art Deco skyscraper, 70 Pine Street, in Manhattan, and lifted rubbings from the elevator doors. These framed rubbings cover two of my windows in such a way as to allow for total privacy, yet still permit daylight to enter the room. I used them on double-hung windows, but you could use this approach to cover a single window, as well.

WHAT YOU NEED

Rubbing paper

Permission letter for rubbing at the site

Materials for making the rubbings

Tape measure

Foam board

Metal framing materials

Plastic for covering rubbing

Silicone rubber glue for attaching picture frame to window sash

Masking tape

Archival adhesive or linen tape for attaching rubbings to foam board

Mat board and mat cutter (optional)

Screws and eyelets

THIS 66-STORY BUILDING, LOCATED AT 70 PINE STREET IN NEW YORK CITY, WAS BUILT AND OWNED BY HENRY L. DOHERTY. BORN IN 1870 IN OHIO, DOHERTY DROPPED OUT OF SCHOOL WHEN HE WAS 10 YEARS OLD TO PEDDLE NEWSPAPERS IN SALOONS. AT 12, HE BECAME AN OFFICE BOY IN A GAS COMPANY, AND QUICKLY WORKED HIS WAY UP TO BECOME BOTH MANAGER AND ENGINEER OF THAT COMPANY. AT 40, HE CAME TO NEW YORK AND FOUNDED THE CITIES SERVICE COMPANY, WHICH EXPLORED OIL AND GAS FIELDS AND SUPPLIED LOCAL USERS. THE REST, AS THEY SAY, IS HISTORY.

WHAT YOU DO

1. Measure your window, and assemble one or two aluminum frames to fit inside the window.

2. Cut foam board to fit into these frames.

3. Mount the rubbing or rubbings onto the foam boards (with or without a mat) using archival adhesive or linen tape. Set them aside.

4. Insert the plastic protective panes into the frames, and tighten the hardware, except for the two corners at the top.

5. If you are working with a double-hung window, glue the two sides and bottom of one aluminum frame to the lower window sash. Secure the frame with masking tape, and leave the glue to cure for 24 hours.

6. Remove the masking tape and the upper section of the aluminum frame and insert your art work into the frame. Replace the upper section of that to sit atop the frame, unfastened.

7. To complete the upper portion of the window, the second aluminum frame should be fully assembled and attached to the window frame (not to the sash) with screws and eyelets, and permitted to hang freely. This enables the lower window to be opened and closed.

8. If you are covering a single window, glue the frame to the lower sash so the window can open.

CAMISOLE WITH GINKGO LEAVES

You can decorate fabric with rubbings of dried leaves or pressed flowers. Then you can turn the fabric into a blouse, vest, or, as shown here, a delicate camisole.

■ WHAT YOU NEED

China silk or other smooth fabric (avoid 100 percent synthetics)

Dried leaves, small ferns, or pressed flowers

Masking tape

White glue

Sheet of clear plastic

Light box (optional)

Wax crayons (lumber crayons or coloring crayons)

Pastel dye sticks

Iron and ironing board

Paper for covering and protecting ironing board and iron

■ WHAT YOU DO

1. Glue the dried leaves onto the plastic sheet.

2. Place the sheet on a light box.

3. Tape the silk to the light box.

4. Use crayons and pastel dye sticks to rub over the leaves. See page 76 for details.

5. Cover your ironing board with scrap paper. Place the silk, with the rubbed images face down, and cover the silk with another piece of paper. Iron the silk as described on page 76.

6. The camisole was made from a pattern purchased from a notions store.

Note: I also made rubbings with sheets, using these same crayons. I once made rubbings of leaves using light-colored linen, and then sewed them into luncheon napkins. These turned out quite well. However, when I worked on black linen I learned that only a white crayon provided enough contrast.

CURTAIN WITH FALLING LEAVES

Sheer curtains are an obvious choice for rubbings. To embellish these lovely curtains, I rubbed dried ferns with fabric crayons in the colors of autumn. For more information about rubbing on fabric, refer to pages 74 to 77.

I chose to make a rubbing on silk to create the material for this shade, but you can make a shade from paper, too. Then I turned the silk over to designer Leah Nall, who transformed it into a lovely lamp shade.

■ WHAT YOU NEED

2 to 3 yards (1.85 to 2.75 m) silk

Dried ferns

Fabric crayons

Light box (optional)

Clip-on lamp shade frame

Bias tape

Measuring tape

Scissors

Iron

Straight pins

Sewing needle

Waxed thread

Fray retardant

2 to 3 yards (1.85 to 2.75 m) lining fabric

Pencil

Ribbon in complementary color

Sewing machine

Designer: Leah Nall

■ WHAT YOU DO

Making the Rubbing

1. Follow the steps for rubbing on silk on page *76*.

Making the Shade

1. Wrap the frame in bias tape.

2. Select the motif for each lamp shade panel by holding the fabric over the frame. Then pin mark each chosen motif (to ensure you can find it again, as well as to prevent accidental cutting).

3. Pin the first motif onto the frame, stretching tightly. Make sure that either the lengthwise or crosswise grain runs straight up the panel.

4. Hand stitch the panel to the wrapped frame, using waxed, doubled thread. Stitches should be no more than ¼ inch (6 mm) apart, with a lockstitch every three or four stitches.

5. Apply fray retardant along the outside edge of the stitches. Let dry.

6. Trim close to the stitching.

7. Repeat steps 3 to 6 for the other panels.

8. On one half of the outside of the shade, pin fit the lining, stretching tightly. Make sure the straight or cross grain runs straight up through the center of the lining.

9. Using a pencil, lightly mark the upper and lower rings, as well as the two opposite struts. In addition, mark the center of the top and bottom rings.

10. Remove the lining from the shade and double check the grain direction.

11. Pin the lining right sides together.

12. Using a stretch overlock setting on your sewing machine, stitch the lining together. Follow just inside the side strut pencil marks, gradually curving the seam deeper through the center of the seam.

13. Apply fray retardant to the outer edge of the stitching. Let dry.

14. Trim close to the stitching.

15. Transfer the upper and lower ring markings to the wrong side of the other lining piece (including center marks).

16. Pin the lining to the inside of the shade, starting with the seams and centers. Work around the top and bottom rings using pencil marks to position the lining correctly. This will be tight.

17. Stitch the lining to the upper and lower rings on the outside edge, using double waxed thread. Stitches should be not more than ¼ inch (6 mm) apart, with a lockstitch every three or four stitches.

18. Apply fray retardant to the outer edge of the stitching. Let it dry.

19. Trim close to the stitching.

20. Measure the circumference of the upper and lower rings, as well as the length of the struts. Add approximately 6 inches (15 cm) to each circumference measurement and 3 inches (8 cm) to each strut measurement to determine the cut lengths needed.

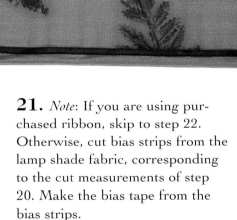

21. *Note*: If you are using purchased ribbon, skip to step 22. Otherwise, cut bias strips from the lamp shade fabric, corresponding to the cut measurements of step 20. Make the bias tape from the bias strips.

22. Using glue or stitches, attach the bias trim (or ribbon) over each strut, being sure to cover the stitches.

23. Using glue or stitches, attach the bias trim (or ribbon) to the top and bottom ring, being sure to cover the stitches. If you are adding a narrow accent, attach this after you have attached the bias trim (or ribbon). Make the join for the trim after all the trim layers have been attached.

PHOTOGRAPHIC TRANSFERS ONTO T-SHIRTS

For this project I visited the Cathedral of Saint John the Divine in New York City. The bull (Taurus) was lifted from the great bronze doors on the outside of the building using the wet method and ink. The fish (Pisces) was lifted from the floor of the cathedral using the dry method and rubbing wax.

■ WHAT YOU NEED

Rubbing paper

Permission letter for rubbing at the site

Materials for making the rubbing

Original rubbing on paper or a photograph of the rubbing, plus any print copy you wish to include

T-shirt, 100 percent cotton or poly/cotton blend*

Iron and ironing board

If you plan to make the transfer yourself, instead of letting a copy shop handle it, you will also need:

> Transfer paper
>
> Computer and printer

*Other items you might consider for photo transfer of rubbings are aprons, tote bags, tablecloths, napkins, and sweatshirts.

■ WHAT YOU DO

1. Select your site and make a dry or wet rubbing on paper.

2. Take the rubbing to a neighborhood copy center that has the equipment required for making a photo transfer onto fabric. Basically, what the machine does is produce a matrix, or master copy, of your rubbing. This is done by running the rubbing through a laser copier onto transfer paper. Transfer paper is treated to produce an iron-on. It is this iron-on that is applied to the T-shirt. Some copy centers are equipped to reproduce your rubbings onto ceramics, mouse pads, place mats, and so on.

Note: If you intend to have your T-shirt produced at a copy center, be certain to specify, in writing, exactly how you want the garment to look upon completion. Signify colors, size of design, fabric content, and shirt size. You might want the design printed on the back of the shirt. That is what I did on the T-shirts shown here.

3. Wash the finished shirt in cold water and tumble dry.

If Using a Home Computer and Printer

A home computer may also be used to make an iron-on transfer of your rubbing. It is necessary to purchase special transfer paper that will work with your particular printer. Instructions come with the packaged transfer paper. Your image will be printed in mirror image (when you use the T-shirt mode through the printer driver) so when you iron it onto the T-shirt, the image will be viewed correctly. Generally, the image will be reproduced satisfactorily if printed on cotton/poly blend fabric.

THE DESIGN AND BUILDING OF THIS REMARKABLE CATHEDRAL OF SAINT JOHN THE DIVINE SPAN 53 YEARS. IN 1888, A DESIGN COMPETITION WAS HELD. AN AURA OF SECRECY SURROUNDED THE COMPETITION, AS ALL ENTRIES HAD TO BE SUBMITTED ANONYMOUSLY AND DESIGNATED BY MOTTOES, I.E., "JERUSALEM THE GOLDEN," "O TEOLOGOS," ETC. IN 1889 A SECOND COMPETITION WAS HELD, LIMITED TO FOUR FINALISTS. THE WINNERS WERE HEINS & LA FARGE. BY THE TIME THE CHOIR WAS COMPLETED, ARCHITECTURAL TASTES HAD CHANGED. HEINS DIED IN 1907, THUS RELEASING THE TRUSTEES FROM THE CONTRACT. RALPH CRAM, WHOSE FIRM HAD SUBMITTED TWO ENTRIES IN THE ORIGINAL COMPETITION, WAS ENGAGED AS A CONSULTANT IN 1911. BUT THE ALTERATIONS THAT BROUGHT THE CHOIR INTO RELATIONSHIP WITH THE NAVE WERE NOT FINISHED UNTIL 1941. THAT FALL, A SERVICE WAS HELD TO CELEBRATE THE OPENING OF THIS PART OF THE CATHEDRAL. FOR CRAM IT WAS A DRAMATIC FINALE; HE DIED 10 MONTHS LATER. CONSTRUCTION FOR COMPLETING THE CATHEDRAL GOES ON TO THIS DAY.

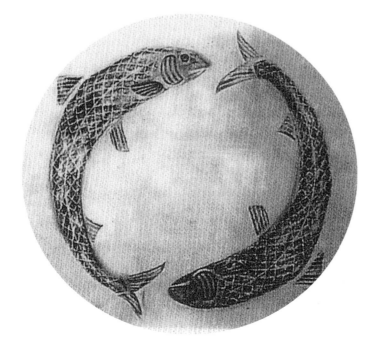

CROWNED ANGEL NEEDLEPOINT PILLOW

Rubbings can also be used as a design to be fully realized in an altogether different form. Talented designer Catherine Reurs used a rubbing I did of an old headstone to create the chart for this stunning pillow. If you want to create your own pattern, follow steps one through four under "Creating the Chart."

Design Size:

*138 stitches wide x 80 stitches high

*Finished size: 10½ inches (27 cm) wide x 6⅛ inches (16 cm) high

■ WHAT YOU NEED

Rubbing on white paper

Fine-point waterproof pens, black and orange

Light box

Piece of 13-mesh needlepoint canvas 15 x 13 inches (38 x 33 cm)

#18 tapestry needle

Fibers (colors and amounts are listed on the color key on page 111)

    Paternayan Persian Tapestry Wool

    Anchor Perle Cotton

    Kreinik metallics

    Madeira metallics

Scissors

Needle threader (optional)

■ WHAT YOU DO

Creating the Chart

1. Trace over your rubbing with a fine-point, black indelible pen.

2. Enlarge or reduce the rubbing on a copier to the size you want.

3. Place the tracing on the light box. Then place the needlepoint canvas on top of the tracing.

4. With the orange pen, transfer the outline of the tracing onto the canvas.

Designer: Catherine Reurs

Pattern and Color Chart on page 111

Stitching the Pillow

1. To stitch this design, follow the chart and fiber color key. Stitch the design in continental stitch, going over one "bar" per stitch. Use 2 plies of Paternayan Persian Tapestry Wool, 1 full strand of Anchor Perle Cotton, 1 strand of

Kreinik #16 braid, and 2 strands of Madeira Glamour in your needle.

2. Stitch the design first, then fill in the background.

3. When all the stitching is complete, finish the design as a pillow or a framed piece.

LEADED STAINED GLASS WINDOW

The basis for this pattern was a heat register in a library in a small Vermont town. When working with stained glass, rubbings can serve more than one purpose; not only can original projects be translated from the rubbings, but repairs of the leaded glass can be accomplished with a rubbing, too. Craftspeople who specialize in the repair of leaded glass use rubbings to manufacture patterns for damaged sections. A precise pattern is traced from an original object by using rubbing paper, graphite, and light pressure. This same technique is also used to pirate patterns. Tiffany glass is sometimes replicated this way.

■ WHAT YOU NEED

Rubbing paper

Permission letter for lifting rubbings at the site

Materials for making a wet rubbing

Glass in colors of your choice

Ruler

Glass cutter

Cardboard

Scissors

Adjustable pliers

Solder

Soldering iron with stainless steel tip

Flux or tinner's solution

Copper foil

Tape

U- or H-shaped lead

*This project assumes experience making leaded, stained glass items. The stained glass shown here was made by a semi-professional craftsperson in Wilmington, Vermont.

■ WHAT YOU DO

1. Make two rubbings of the design you wish to use.

2. Cut one rubbing to use as a pattern for the cardboard shapes from which the glass pieces will be cut.

3. The second rubbing is used to lay out the cut glass pieces and to define the design. The heat register from which this stained glass was created had many small segments. After laying the pieces out on the second rubbing, I decided to take some liberties with the original design by consolidating some of the smaller pieces into

Rubbing of heat register, Pettee Memorial Library, Wilmington, Vermont

larger shapes. An alternative strategy is to place the pattern under the glass. If it is transparent enough, trace the outline of the pattern onto the glass with a grease pencil. Cut on this line with the glass cutter. When you are working with many glass pieces, allow 1/16 to 1/8 inch (1.5 to 3 mm) for the width of the lead. Professionals use double-bladed glass cutting knives.

4. When cutting the glass, lay it on a flat, resilient surface. The cutter should pass over the line only once, as a light scoring is all that is necessary.

5. To break the glass along the cut, lift the end of the glass and place the handle of the glass cutter under the score line.

6. Apply downward pressure manually on either side of this line. The glass should break cleanly. It is helpful to tap the bottom side of the glass along the line of the score mark to facilitate separating the two pieces.

Note: To achieve accurate results with the glass cutter, it is necessary to keep the blade in excellent condition. Cutting will be smoother if you store the blade in light oil or kerosene. The lubricant reduces heat and friction along the cutting line, improving your chances for a smoother line.

7. As the pieces are cut, assemble them on the second rubbing.

8. Once all the pieces are cut out, join them with lead and soldering. Using longer pieces of lead will reduce the number of joints to be soldered.

9. Firmly press the lead onto the edges of the glass so that no light is visible between the glass and the lead. Be careful to not melt the joints by permitting the soldering iron to remain on them for too long.

For this project I visited the Pettee Memorial Library in Wilmington, Vermont. The library was one of the first in the state, and its origins date back to 1796. It started in the form of a club, the Wilmington Social Library. To join the association, each member paid an initial fee of $1.50, and then annual dues of 50 cents. The books were kept in one member's home while another acted as librarian. Fines for overdue books were determined by the thickness of the book. One penny a day was charged for a small one and the charge increased by half a penny for the next increment in size. The library still has the original constitution and bylaws, dated December 31, 1795, written in a composition book.

You may find many of the materials needed to complete the projects in this book at local arts- and crafts-supply stores. The following list of mail-order sources has been provided to help you in the event that you are unable to find a particular product in your area.

United States

Aiko's Art Materials Import
3347 N. Clark St.
Chicago, IL 60657
Tel: (312) 404-5600

Japanese handmade papers and art supplies

Daniel Smith, Inc.
4150 1st Avenue S
P.O. Box 84268
Seattle, WA 98124
Tel: (800) 426-6740

Extensive selection of papers and inks

Meininger
499 Broadway
Denver, CO 80203
Tel: (800) 950-2787

Website: www.meininger.com

Full range of art supplies including inks and exotic papers. Project ideas and catalog available on their website.

New York Central Art Supply, Inc.
62 Third Avenue
New York City, NY 10003
Tel: (212) 477-2513
and (800) 950-6111
Fax: (212) 475-2513

Specialists in fine art papers. They publish an extensive catalog on this subject and sell sample books of their papers. They also stock the rubbing supplies mentioned in this book.

Pearl Paint Co. Inc.
308 Canal Street
New York, NY 10013
Tel: (212) 431-7932
and (800) 451-7327
Fax: (800) PEARL-91

Discounted art supplies, including powdered graphite and many of the supplies mentioned in this book. Fine arts catalog.

Yasutomo and Company
490 Eccles Avenue
South San Francisco, CA 94080-1901
Tel: (415) 737-8888
and (800) 262-6454
Fax: (415) 737-8877

Oriental art materials, including Sumi inks in colors, suzuri stones, and some oriental papers. Catalog is divided into three categories: craft, Western art, and oriental art.

Oldstone Enterprises
1 De Angelo Drive
Bedford, MA 01730-1808
Tel: (781) 271-0480
Fax: (781) 271-0499

Rubbing waxes in several colors, including gold and silver. Aqaba paper in both black and white, and a general line of rubbing supplies. Catalog.

Nasco Art and Crafts
901 Janesville Avenue
Fort Atkinson, WI 53538-0901
Tel: (920) 563-2446
and (800) 558-9595
Fax: (920) 563-8296

Replica fish printing kits, fabric crayons, and general variety of arts and especially crafts products. Catalog.

Gravestone Artwear™ Collection
P.O. Box 141
York Harbor, Maine 03911
Tel: (207) 351-1434
and (800) 564-4310
Fax: (207) 363-3268

Variety of New England and Celtic rubbings hand-screened onto T-shirts, soap, rubber stamps, window decals, velvet dresses, scarfs, and other items. Catalog.

Australia

Oxford Art Supplies Pty. Ltd
221-223 Oxford Street
Darlinghurst NSW 2010
Sydney, Australia
Tel: (612) 9360 4066

Website: www.oxfordart.com.au

E-mail: orders@oxfordart.com.au

Online catalog of art supplies including papers, fabric paints and pastels.

Canada

Bisbees
719B Yates Street
Victoria, BC V8W 1L6
Canada
Tel: (250) 385-4965

Website: www.waxworld.com/bisbees

Catalog of ready-made brass rubbings for sale. Visit their shop to lift rubbings from their collection of 60 medieval monumental brasses.

England

White Winds Moorshall Cottages
Kingston St. Michael
Chippenham
Wilts, England SN146JX
Tel./ Fax: 01249 750667

Specialist suppliers of monumental brass facsimiles and reduced scale brasses from England and the Continent. Illustrated, biographical catalog also includes tea towels and T-shirts (black and white). Brass rubbing materials including Astral Brass Rubbing Waxes and English detail paper in black and white. Also give advice and help for setting up your own brass rubbing center. Catalogs, wholesale and retail.

The London Brass Rubbing Centre
St. Martin-in-the-Fields Church
Trafalgar Square
London WC2N 4JJ
Tel: 0171 930 9306

Ready-made brass rubbings, instruction, and supplies, as well as gifts inspired by the brasses.

Monumental brass facsimile rubbing

There are many brass rubbing centers in England.
A list of their locations may be obtained free of cost
from The British Tourist Authority.
In the U.S., the Authority is located at:

551 Fifth Avenue
New York, New York 10017
Tel: (212) 986-2200

Rubbing Techniques

Andrew, Laye. *Creative Rubbings.* New York: Watson Guptill Publications, 1967.

Beedell, Suzanne. *Brasses and Brass Rubbing.* Edinburgh: John Bartholomew & Son Ltd, 1973.

Betram, Jerome. *Brasses and Brass Rubbing in England.* Devon: David & Charles, 1971.

Bodor, John J. *Rubbings and Textures: A Graphic Technique.* New York: Reinhold, 1968.

Busby, Richard J. *Beginner's Guide to Brass Rubbing.* London: Pelham Books, 1971.

Cook, Malcolm. *Discovering Brasses and Brass Rubbing.* Hertforshire, England, 1970.

Firestein, Cecily Barth. *Rubbing Craft.* New York: Quick Fox, 1977.

Friede, E. P. *Rubbings from Rock Engravings: Discussion of a Recent Method. Africana Notes and News.* Johannesburg: Cape Times Limited, March 1955 Vol. XI, No. 6.

Hiyama, Yoshio. *Gyotaku: Art and Technique of the Japanese Fish Print.* Seattle: University of Seattle Press 1964.

Marks Glen K. *Oldstone's Guide to Creative Rubbing.* Boston: Oldstone Enterprises, 1973.

McGeer, William J. A. *Reproducing Relief Surfaces: Handbook of Rubbing, Dabbing, Casting and Daubing.* Concord, MA: Minute Man Printing Corp, 1972.

Pluckrose, Henry. *Introducing Crayon Techniques.* New York: Watson Guptill, 1967.

Skinner, Michael K. *How to Make Rubbings.* London: Studio Vista/Van-Nostrand Reinhold, 1972.

Collections and Descriptions: Rubbings, Brasses, Gravestones

Bartram, Alan. *Tombstone Lettering in the British Isles.* London: Lund Humphries, 1978.

Clayton, Muriel M. *A Catalogue of Rubbings of Brasses and Incised Slabs.* London: Her Majesty's Stationery Office, 1968.

De Sola Pool, David. *Portraits Etched in Stone: Early Jewish Settlers 1682–1851.* New York: Columbia University Press, 1952.

Ellis, Nancy & Parker Hayden. *Here Lies America: A Collection of Notable Graves.* New York: Hawthorn Books, 1978.

Forbes, Harriette M. *Gravestones of Early New England and the Men Who Made Them:1653–1800.* New Jersey: Pine Press, 1955.

Gillon, Edmund V. Jr. *Early New England Gravestone Rubbings.* New York: Dover Publications, 1966.

Greenhill, Frank A. *Incised Effigial Slabs: Study of Engraved Stone Memorials in Latin Christendom 1100–1700.* London: Faber & Faber, 1976.

Jacobs, G. Walker. *Stop and Cast an Eye: Guide to stones & rubbings.* Marblehead, MA: Oldstone Enterprises, 1972.

Kahn, Phd., Roy Max. *Gravestones of the United States, 1648–1850: Photos of Rubbings Done by Him in New England.* Berkeley, 1979.

Kriger, Malcolm D. *The Peaceable Kingdom in Hartsdale: A Celebration of Pets and their People.* New York. Rosywick Press, 1983.

Kull, Andrew. *New England Cemeteries: A Collector's Guide.* Brattleboro: Stephen Greene Press, 1975.

Ludwig, Allan I. *Graven Images: New England Stone Carving and its Symbols, 1650–1815.* Middletown: Wesleyan University Press, 1966.

Morris, Malcolm. *Brass Rubbing.* New York: Dover Publications, 1965.

Page-Phillips, John. *Macklin's Monumental Brasses.* New York: Praeger Inc., 1969.

Stained glass door in the Loew's Paradise Theater, Bronx, New York

Smith, Elmer L. *Early American Gravestone Designs: Folk Art of New Jersey, Maryland, Pennsylvania and Virginia.* Lebanon: Applied Arts Publishers, 1972.

Tashjian, Ann and Dickran. *Memorials for Children of Change: Art of Early New England Stone Carving.* Middletown: Wesleyan University Press, 1974.

Trivick, Henry. *The Craft and Design of Monumental Brasses.* New York: The Humanities Press, 1969.

Wasserman, Emily. *Gravestone Designs.* New York: Dover Publications, 1972.

Williams, Melvin G. *The Last Word: The Lure and Lore of Early New England Graveyards.* Boston: Oldstone Enterprises, 1973.

Wust, Kalus. *Folk Art in Stone.* Edinburg, VA. West Virginia Shenandoah History. 1970.

Architecture and History

Goldstone, Harmon H. and Darymple. *History Preserved: A Guide to New York City Landmarks and Historic Districts.* New York: Simon & Schuster, 1974.

Jackson, Kenneth T., Ed. *The Encyclopedia of New York City.* New Haven: Yale University Press, 1995.

Wolter, Carlo. *Wilmington Library Dates from One of the State's First.* Bennington Banner, July 24, 1964.

Parker, Ann & Neal, Avon. *A Portfolio of Rubbings: Burying Grounds of New England.* Woodstock: Elm Tree Press, 1963.

Pommeranz-Liedtke, Gerhard. *Die Weisheit der Kunst: Chinesische Steinabreibungen.* Germany: Insel-Verlag, 1963.

Pritchard, Violet. *English Medieval Graffiti.* Cambridge: Cambridge University Press, 1967.

Schwartzman, Arnold. *Graven Images: Graphic Motifs of the Jewish Gravestone.* New York: Harry N. Abrams Inc., 1993.

ACKNOWLEDGMENTS

DAVID ALDERA
Manager, paper department,
New York Central Art Supply Company

MYRON AMER, Esq.

PAULETTE CHERNACK
Gravestone Artwear™

The late ALEXANDER CHOWSKI
for his stained glass project

STEPHEN K. FIRESTEIN

THOM GAINES
for creating the room divider

RACHEL GINSBURG

DAVE HEINHECKER
Binney & Smith

FAISAL G. KHAN
for his help with the
photo transfers for the T-shirts

CALDER MAXWELL
Tailor, for sewing the camisole

VIVIAN MILES
Director, Pettee Memorial Library,
Wilmington, Vermont

DEBORAH MORGENTHAL
my editor at Lark Books

LEAH NALL
for creating the silk lamp shade

TERESA PIJON
Albuquerque, New Mexico,
for her information on petroglyphs

CATHERINE REURS
for creating the needlepoint pillow

OREN SLOR
Photographer

HEATHER SMITH
for creating the gift paper and frame,
and for demonstrating rubbing techniques

STEVE STEINBERG
Owner, New York Central Art Supply Company

TERRY TAYLOR
for creating the note cards

KERRY JOHN UPCHURCH
of Whitewinds, Chippenham, England

JENNIFER VICKERY
Public Affairs Assistant,
Woolworth Corporation

ANN WILSHIN
Assistant Manager,
The London Brass Rubbing Centre,
Saint Martin-in-the-Fields Church

Color Key for Angel Needlepoint Pillow © Catherine Reurs 1998   Enlarge 142%

	Color	Amount	What to Use
W =	Madeira Glamour metallic 2400	1 spool	2 strands
I =	Paternayan Persian Tapestry Wool 213	5 yards (4.6 m)	2 strands
R =	Anchor Perle Cotton #3 47	1 skein	1 strand
△ =	Anchor Perle Cotton #3 333	1 skein	1 strand
/ =	Anchor Perle Cotton #3 302	1 skein	1 strand
Ŋ =	Anchor Perle Cotton #3 244	1 skein	1 strand
← =	Anchor Perle Cotton #3 132	1 skein	1 strand
∩ =	Anchor Perle Cotton #3 112	1 skein	1 strand
Ǝ =	Anchor Perle Cotton #3 98	1 skein	1 strand
■ =	Kreinik #16 Braid 205C (metallic)	1 spool	1 strand
T =	Madeira Glamour metallic 2425	1 spool	2 strands
■ =	Paternayan Persian Tapestry Wool 220	10 yards (9 m)	2 strands
· =	Paternayan Persian Tapestry Wool 221 and 222	20 yards (18 m) per color	1 strand per color together in your needle
▶ =	Paternayan Persian Tapestry Wool 221	5 yards (4.6 m)	2 strands
L =	Anchor Perle Cotton #3 110	1 spool	1 strand